THE MYSTICAL LORE OF

PRECIOUS STONES

Being a Combination of Two Histories, "The
Curious Lore of Precious Stones," 1913, and
"The Magic of Jewels and Charms," 1915

VOLUME I

THE CLASSIC WRITINGS OF

GEORGE FREDERICK KUNZ

A.M., PH.D., D.SC.

ILLUSTRATED

NEWCASTLE PUBLISHING CO., INC.
NORTH HOLLYWOOD, CALIFORNIA
1986

WITH HEARTFELT APPRECIATION OF THE NOBLE SPIRIT THAT CON-
CEIVED AND FOUNDED THE MORGAN-TIFFANY COLLECTION OF GEMS
AND THE MORGAN-BEMENT COLLECTIONS OF MINERALS AND METEOR-
ITES OF THE AMERICAN MUSEUM OF NATURAL HISTORY, AND THE
MORGAN COLLECTION OF THE MUSÉE D'HISTOIRE NATURELLE OF
PARIS, AND WHOSE KINDLY ADVICE AND ENCOURAGEMENT HAVE
DONE SO MUCH FOR THE PRECIOUS STONE ART, THIS VOLUME
IS RESPECTFULLY DEDICATED TO THE MEMORY OF THE LATE

J. PIERPONT MORGAN

A NEWCASTLE GEM AND CRYSTAL CLASSIC
First Paperback Printing August 1986
9 8 7 6 5 4 3 2 1
Printed in the United States of America

Preface

THE love of precious stones is deeply implanted in the human heart, and the cause of this must be sought not only in their coloring and brilliancy but also in their durability. All the fair colors of flowers and foliage, and even the blue of the sky and the glory of the sunset clouds, only last for a short time, and are subject to continual change, but the sheen and coloration of precious stones are the same to-day as they were thousands of years ago and will be for thousands of years to come. In a world of change, this permanence has a charm of its own that was early appreciated.

The object of this book is to indicate and illustrate the various ways in which precious stones have been used at different times and among different peoples, and more especially to explain some of the curious ideas and fancies that have gathered around them. Many of these ideas may seem strange enough to us now, and yet when we analyze them we find that they have their roots either in some intrinsic quality of the stones or else in an instinctive appreciation of their symbolical significance. Through manifold transformations this symbolism has persisted to the present day.

The same thing may be said in regard to the various superstitions connected with gems. Our scientific knowledge of cause and effect may prevent us from accepting any of the fanciful notions of the physicians and astrologers of the olden time; nevertheless, the possession of a necklace or a ring adorned with brilliant diamonds, fair pearls, warm, glowing rubies, or celestial-hued sapphires will to-day make a woman's heart beat faster and bring a blush of pleasure to her cheek. Life will seem better worth living to her; and, indeed, this is no delusion, for life is what our thought makes it, and joy is born of gratified desire. Hence nothing that contributes to increasing the sum of innocent pleasures should be disdained; and surely no pleasure can be more innocent and justifiable than that inspired by the possession of beautiful natural objects.

The author, who possesses what is believed to be the most comprehensive private library on this subject, has obtained many references from material which he has been gathering during the past twenty-five years. Many of the types exist in the collection of folk-lore precious stones exhibited at the World's Columbian Exposition in 1893, and now in the Field Museum of Natural History in Chicago. Other types are drawn from the Morgan Collection exhibited at the Paris Expositions of 1889 and 1900, which, with additions, is now in Morgan Hall, in the American Museum of Natural History, New York City.

Other prominent references are the collection of precious stones in the California Midwinter Memorial Museum, in Golden Gate Park, San Francisco; the Tiffany collection of precious stones, exhibited at the Atlanta Exposition of 1894, now in the National Museum in Washington; the collection exhibited at the Pan-American Exposition, and presented to the Musée d'Histoire Naturelle, in Paris, by the late J. Pierpont Morgan; the collection exhibited at the exposition held in Portland, Oregon, in 1905; and the collection of gems and precious stones exhibited at the Jamestown Exposition, 1907. All of these collections, either entirely or very largely, have been formed by the author.

Some references to sentiment connected with precious stones are embodied in the little work, now in its 21st

THE MYSTICAL LORE OF

PRECIOUS STONES

Being a Combination of Two Histories, ''The Curious Lore of Precious Stones,'' 1913, and ''The Magic of Jewels and Charms,'' 1915

VOLUME I

THE CLASSIC WRITINGS OF

GEORGE FREDERICK KUNZ

A.M., PH.D., D.SC.

ILLUSTRATED

NEWCASTLE PUBLISHING CO., INC.
NORTH HOLLYWOOD, CALIFORNIA
1986

WITH HEARTFELT APPRECIATION OF THE NOBLE SPIRIT THAT CON-
CEIVED AND FOUNDED THE MORGAN-TIFFANY COLLECTION OF GEMS
AND THE MORGAN-BEMENT COLLECTIONS OF MINERALS AND METEOR-
ITES OF THE AMERICAN MUSEUM OF NATURAL HISTORY, AND THE
MORGAN COLLECTION OF THE MUSÉE D'HISTOIRE NATURELLE OF
PARIS, AND WHOSE KINDLY ADVICE AND ENCOURAGEMENT HAVE
DONE SO MUCH FOR THE PRECIOUS STONE ART, THIS VOLUME
IS RESPECTFULLY DEDICATED TO THE MEMORY OF THE LATE

J. PIERPONT MORGAN

A NEWCASTLE GEM AND CRYSTAL CLASSIC
First Paperback Printing August 1986
9 8 7 6 5 4 3 2 1
Printed in the United States of America

Preface

THE love of precious stones is deeply implanted in the human heart, and the cause of this must be sought not only in their coloring and brilliancy but also in their durability. All the fair colors of flowers and foliage, and even the blue of the sky and the glory of the sunset clouds, only last for a short time, and are subject to continual change, but the sheen and coloration of precious stones are the same to-day as they were thousands of years ago and will be for thousands of years to come. In a world of change, this permanence has a charm of its own that was early appreciated.

The object of this book is to indicate and illustrate the various ways in which precious stones have been used at different times and among different peoples, and more especially to explain some of the curious ideas and fancies that have gathered around them. Many of these ideas may seem strange enough to us now, and yet when we analyze them we find that they have their roots either in some intrinsic quality of the stones or else in an instinctive appreciation of their symbolical significance. Through manifold transformations this symbolism has persisted to the present day.

The same thing may be said in regard to the various superstitions connected with gems. Our scientific knowledge of cause and effect may prevent us from accepting any of the fanciful notions of the physicians and astrologers of the olden time; nevertheless, the possession of a necklace or a ring adorned with brilliant diamonds, fair pearls, warm, glowing rubies, or celestial-hued sapphires will to-day make a woman's heart beat faster

and bring a blush of pleasure to her cheek. Life will
seem better worth living to her; and, indeed, this is no
delusion, for life is what our thought makes it, and joy
is born of gratified desire. Hence nothing that contributes to increasing the sum of innocent pleasures
should be disdained; and surely no pleasure can be more
innocent and justifiable than that inspired by the possession of beautiful natural objects.

The author, who possesses what is believed to be the
most comprehensive private library on this subject, has
obtained many references from material which he has
been gathering during the past twenty-five years. Many
of the types exist in the collection of folk-lore precious
stones exhibited at the World's Columbian Exposition in
1893, and now in the Field Museum of Natural History
in Chicago. Other types are drawn from the Morgan Collection exhibited at the Paris Expositions of 1889 and
1900, which, with additions, is now in Morgan Hall, in the
American Museum of Natural History, New York City.

Other prominent references are the collection of precious stones in the California Midwinter Memorial
Museum, in Golden Gate Park, San Francisco; the
Tiffany collection of precious stones, exhibited at the
Atlanta Exposition of 1894, now in the National Museum
in Washington; the collection exhibited at the Pan-
American Exposition, and presented to the Musée
d'Histoire Naturelle, in Paris, by the late J. Pierpont
Morgan; the collection exhibited at the exposition held
in Portland, Oregon, in 1905; and the collection of gems
and precious stones exhibited at the Jamestown Exposition, 1907. All of these collections, either entirely
or very largely, have been formed by the author.

Some references to sentiment connected with precious
stones are embodied in the little work, now in its 21st

edition, entitled: "Natal Stones, Sentiments and Superstitions Associated with Precious Stones," compiled by
the writer, who has examined nearly all the principal collections in the United States, Europe, Mexico, Canada, and
Asiatic Russia.

For courtesies, information and illustrations, I am in-
debted to the following, to whom my thanks are due:

Prof. Taw Sein Ko, Superintendent of the Archæo-
logical Survey, of Burma; Dr. T. Wada, of Tokyo, Japan;
Dr. G. O. Clerc, President of the Société Ouralienne des
Amis des Sciences Naturelles, Ekaterinebourg, Russia;
Dr. Charles Braddock, late Medical Inspector to the King
of Siam; Sir Charles Hercules Reed, Curator of Archæ-
ology, and Dr. Ernest A. Wallis Budge, Egyptologist,
British Museum, London; A. W. Feavearyear, Esq., Lon-
don; Dr. Salomon Reinach, Director of the Archæological
Museum of St. Germain-en-Laye, France; Prof. Giuseppe
Belucci, of the University of Perugia; Dr. Peter Jessen,
Librarian of the Kunstgewerbe Museum, of Berlin; Miss
Belle DaCosta Green; Dr. Frederick Hirth, Chinese Pro-
fessor, Columbia University, New York; Dr. Clark
Wissler, Curator of Archæology, Dr. L. P. Gratacap,
Curator of Mineralogy, American Museum of Natural
History; Dr. Berthold Laufer, Oriental Archæologist,
and Dr. Oliver C. Farrington, Curator of Geology and
Mineralogy, Field Museum of Natural History, Chicago;
Hereward Carrington, Esq., Psychist, New York; Dr. W.
Hayes Ward, Archæologist and Babylonian Scholar; Mrs.
Henry Draper, New York; H. W. Kent, Esq., Metro-
politan Museum of Art, New York City; Consul General
Moser, Colombo, Ceylon; W. W. Blake, Mexico City, who
has done so much to encourage Mexican archæological
investigation; the late A. Damour, of Paris, the great
pioneer of mineralogical archæology; the late Dr. A. B.

Meyer, of Dresden, who, more than anyone else, proved that the *Nephritfrage* or the jade question was to be solved by chemical and mineralogical investigation; the late Rajah Sir Sourindro Mohun Tagore, of Calcutta; and Dr. A. M. Lythgoe, Egyptologist, Metropolitan Museum of Art.

G. F. K.

SEPTEMBER, 1913.

Contents

VOLUME II DESCRIBES:

    RELIGIOUS USES OF PRECIOUS STONES, PAGAN, HEBREW,
       AND CHRISTIAN,
    THE HIGH-PRIEST'S BREASTPLATE,
    BIRTH-STONES,
    PLANETARY AND ASTRAL INFLUENCES OF PRECIOUS STONES,
    THERAPEUTIC USE OF PRECIOUS AND SEMI-PRECIOUS STONES.

The Curious Lore of Precious Stones

I

Superstitions and Their Sources

FROM the earliest times in man's history gems and precious stones have been held in great esteem. They have been found in the monuments of prehistoric peoples, and not alone the civilization of the Pharaohs, of the Incas, or of the Montezumas invested these brilliant things from Nature's jewel casket with a significance beyond the mere suggestion of their intrinsic properties.

The magi, the wise men, the seers, the astrologers of the ages gone by found much in the matter of gems that we have nearly come to forgetting. With them each gem possessed certain planetary attractions peculiar to itself, certain affinities with the various virtues, and a zodiacal concordance with the seasons of the year. Moreover, these early sages were firm believers in the influence of gems in one's nativity,—that the evil in the world could be kept from contaminating a child properly protected by wearing the appropriate talismanic, natal, and zodiacal gems. Indeed, folklorists are wont to wonder whether the custom of wearing gems in jewelry did not originate in the talismanic idea instead of in the idea of mere additional adornment.

The influence exerted by precious stones was assumed in medieval times without question, but when the spirit of investigation was aroused in the Renaissance period, an effort was made to find a reason of some sort for the traditional beliefs. Strange as it may seem to us, there was little disposition to doubt that the influence existed; this was taken for granted, and all the mental effort expended was devoted to finding some plausible explanation as to how precious stones became endowed with their strange and mystic virtues, and how these virtues acted in modifying the character, health, or fortunes of the wearer.

When the existence of miracles is acknowledged, there will always be a tendency to regard every singular and unaccountable happening as a miracle; that is to say, as something that occurs outside of, or in spite of, the laws of nature. We even observe this tendency at work in our own time. As regards visual impressions, for instance, if a child of lively imagination enters a half-lighted room and sees a bundle of clothes lying in a corner, the indistinct outline of this mass may be transformed to his mind into the form of a wild animal. The child does not really see an animal, but his fear has given a definite outline and character to the indefinite image printed on the retina.

The writer has always sought to investigate anything strange and apparently unaccountable which has been brought to his notice, but he can truly say he has never found the slightest evidence of anything transcending the acknowledged laws of nature. Still, when we consider the marvellous secrets that have been revealed to us by science and the yet more wonderful things that will be revealed to us in the future, we are tempted to think that there may be something in the old beliefs, some residuum of fact, susceptible indeed of explanation, but very different from what a crass scepticism supposes it to be. Above all, the results of the investigations now pursued in relation to the group of phe-

nomena embraced under the designation of telepathy,—
the subconscious influence of one mind over an absent or
distant mind,—and the wireless transmission of power
in wireless telegraphy and telephony, may go far to make
us hesitate before condemning as utterly preposterous
many of the tales of enchantment and magical influence.
If the unconscious will of one individual can affect the
thoughts and feelings of another individual at a great
distance and without the intervention of any known
means of communication, as is confidently asserted by
many competent investigators in the domain of telepathy, their claims being supported by many strange
happenings, perhaps the result of coincidence, but possibly due to the operation of some unknown law, does
this not give a color of verity to the statements regarding
the ancient magicians and their spells?

Auto-suggestion may also afford an explanation of
much that is mysterious in the effects attributed to
precious stones, for if the wearer be firmly convinced
that the gem he is wearing produces certain results, this
conviction will impress itself upon his thought and hence
upon his very organism. He will really experience the
influence, and the effects will manifest themselves just
as powerfully as though they were caused by vibrations
or emanations from the material body of the stone.

All this may serve to explain the persistence of the
belief in magic arts. A few hundred years ago, a Hungarian woman was accused of having murdered two or
three hundred young girls, and at her trial she confessed
that her object was to use the blood of her victims to
renew her youth and beauty, for the blood of innocent
virgins was supposed to have wonderful properties. In
some parts of England to-day there is a superstitious
belief that an article of clothing worn by a person, or

anything he has habitually used, absorbs a portion of his individuality. Therefore, it sometimes happens that a handkerchief, for instance, will be stolen and pinned down beneath the waters of a stream on a toad, the pins marking the name of the enemy, the belief being that as this cloth wastes away, so will the body of him who had worn it. In medieval and later times this was the common practice of the sorcerers, although they frequently composed a wax figure rudely resembling the person against whom the spell was directed, and then thrust pins into this figure or allowed it to melt away before a slow fire. The enchantment of the sorcerer was supposed to have caused some essence of the personality to enter into the image, and therefore the living and breathing being felt sympathetically the effects of the ill-treatment inflicted upon its counterfeit.

The persistence of the most cruel and unnatural practices of old-time sorcery is illustrated by the fact that only a few years ago, in the island of Cuba, three women were condemned to death for murdering a white baby so as to use the heart and blood as a cure for diseases. Four other women were sentenced to from fourteen to twenty years' imprisonment as accomplices. When such things happen in Cuba, it is not surprising that in half-civilized Hayti similar crimes are committed. Here the Voodoo priests and priestesses, *papalois* and *mamalois* (papa-kings and mama-queens) require from time to time a human sacrifice to appease their serpent-god. One strange case is related where a stupefying potion, inducing a state of apparent death, was secretly administered to a sick man. When the attending physician pronounced him dead, he was duly interred; but, two days after, the grave was found open and the body had disappeared. The Voodoo worshippers had carried the man away so as to revive him and then sacrifice him at their fearful rites.

In a poem addressed to Marguerite de Valois,—"La Marguerite des Marguerites," as she was called,—by Jean de la Taille de Bondaroy,[1] we read of the diamond that it came from gold and from the sun. But we are told that not only are precious stones endowed with life, they also are subject to disease, old age, and death; "they even take offence if an injury be done to them, and become rough and pale." The sickness of the pearl has been a theme for centuries, and in many cases is only fancied. It is but a subterfuge or deception for a lady to remark that her pearls have sickened; by referring to this sickness, her friends are naturally led to believe that at one time her pearls were fine, perfect ones, when in reality they may never have been so.

The opinion given in 1609, by Anselmus De Boot, court physician to Rudolph II of Germany, regarding the power inherent in certain precious stones,[2] embodies the ideas on this subject held by many of the enlightened minds of that period.

The supernatural and acting cause is God, the good angel and the evil one; the good by the will of God, and the evil by His permission. . . . What God can do by Himself, He could do also by means of ministers, good and bad angels, who, by special grace of God and for the preservation of men, are enabled to enter precious stones and to guard men from dangers or procure some special grace for them. However, as we may not affirm anything positive touching the presence of angels in gems, to repose trust in them, or to ascribe undue powers to them, is more especially pleasing to the spirit of evil, who transforms

---

[1] Jean de la Taille de Bondaroy, "Le Blason de la Marguerite," Paris, 1574.

[2] De Boot, "Gemmarum et lapidum historia," lib. i, cap. 25, Lug. Bat., 1636, pp. 87, 91.

himself into an angel of light, steals into the substance of the little gem, and works such wonders by it that some people do not place their trust in God but in a gem, and seek to obtain from it what they should ask of God alone. Thus it is perhaps the spirit of evil which exercises its power on us through the turquoise, teaching us, little by little, that safety is not to be sought from God but from a gem.

In the next chapter of his work, De Boot, while extolling the remedial power of a certain group of stones, insists upon the falsity of many of the superstitions regarding these objects.[3]

That gems or stones, when applied to the body, exert an action upon it, is so well proven by the experience of many persons, that any one who doubts this must be called over-bold. We have proof of this power in the carnelian, the hematite, and the jasper, all of which when applied, check hemorrhage. . . . However, it is very necessary to observe that many virtues not possessed by gems are falsely ascribed to them.

Paracelsus, the gifted and brilliant thinker, scientist, and, we must probably add, charlatan of the sixteenth century, whose really extraordinary mental endowment was largely wasted in the effort to impress his followers with the idea that he had a mystic control over supernatural agencies, was the owner of a talismanic jewel which he asserted to be the dwelling-place of a powerful spirit named " Azoth." Some old portraits of the philosopher, or pseudo-philosopher, figure him wearing this jewel, in whose virtues we may fairly doubt that he himself believed, but which furnished part of the paraphernalia be freely employed to gain influence over the credulous.[4]

---

[3] De Boot, " Gemmarum et lapidum historia," lib. i, cap. 26, Lug. Bat., 1636, p. 103.

[4] Mackey, " Memoirs of Extraordinary Popular Delusions," London, n. d., p. 144.

The following passage from the ''Faithful Lapidary'' of Thomas Nicols,[5] who wrote in the middle of the seventeenth century, illustrates the prevailing opinion in England at that time as to the virtues of precious stones:

Perfectionem effectûs contineri in causa. But it cannot truly be so spoken of gemms and pretious stones, the effects of which, by Lapidists are said to be, the making of men rich and eloquent, to preserve men from thunder and lightning, from plagues and diseases, to move dreams, to procure sleep, to foretell things to come, to make men wise, to strengthen memory, to procure honours, to hinder fascinations and witchcrafts, to hinder slothfulness, to put courage into men, to keep men chaste, to increase friendship, to hinder difference and dissention, and to make men invisible, as is feigned by the Poet concerning Gyges ring, and affirmed by Albertus and others concerning the *ophthalmius lapis,* and many other strange things are affirmed of them and ascribed to them, which are contrary to the nature of gemms, and which they as they are materiall, mixt, inanimate bodies neither know nor can effect, by the properties and faculties of their own constitutions: because they being naturall causes, can produce none other but naturall effects, such as are all the ordinary effects of gemms: that is, such effects as flow from their elementary matter, from their temper, form and essence; such as are the operations of hot and cold, and of all the first qualities, and all such accidents as do arise from the commixtion of the first qualities: such as are hardnesse, heavinesse, thicknesse, colour, and tast. These all are the naturall faculties of gemms, and these are the known effects of the union of their matter, and of the operation of the first qualities one upon another.

The long-continued concentration of vision on an object tends to produce a partial paralysis of certain functions of the brain. This effect may be noted in the helplessness of a bird when its gaze is fixed upon the glittering eyes of a serpent, or in the unwilling obedience yielded by a lion or some other wild animal when forced to look into the intent eyes of its trainer. In the same way those who gaze for a long time and without inter-

---

[5] Nicols, " Faithful Lapidary," London, 1659, pp. 32, 33.

ruption on a crystal or glass ball, on an opal, a moon-stone, a sapphire, or a cat's-eye, may become partially hypnotized or even fall into a profound sleep. The condition induced, whether it be that of semi-trance, of hypnotism, or simply due to the imaginative workings of the brain, is believed to give an insight into the future. This hypnotic effect is probably caused by some gleam or point of light in the stone, attracting and fixing the beholder's gaze. The moonstone, the star sapphire, and the cat's-eye are all gems which possess a moving light, a moving line, or three crossed lines, and they are believed by the Orientals to be gems of good luck. Indeed, it is supposed in the East that a living spirit dwells within these stones, a spirit potent for good.

Superstitious fancies bear the same relation to truth that the shadow of a form does to the form itself. We know that the shadow has no substantial existence, and yet we know equally well that it is cast by some real body; in the same way we may be sure that, however foolish a superstition may appear to be, it has some foundation in fact. Indeed, superstition is associated with the highest attribute of the human mind,—imagination. The realities about us gain much of their charm from sentiment, and all that is great in art and literature owes its being to the transforming energy of pure imagination. Morbid imagination, on the other hand, distorts and degrades the impressions it receives and produces only unlovely or ignoble forms and ideas.

Sentiment may best be expressed as the feeling of one who, on a warm summer's day, is rowing along a shady brook or resting in some sylvan dell, with nothing to interfere with his tranquil mood and nothing to spur him on to action; thus he has only suggestions of hope and indulges in rosy views of life. Reality, on the other hand, may be likened to a crisp winter's morning when one is filled with exhilaration, conscious of the tingle of the cold, but comfortable in the knowledge of wearing a tightly-buttoned garment which will afford protection should the elements become disturbing. Superstition, lastly, can be said to resemble a dark, cold, misty night, when the moon is throwing malevolent shadows which are weird and distorted, while the cold seems to seize one by the throat and arouse a passionate desire to free one's self from its grip in some way, to change a horrible nightmare into a pleasant dream.

In the early part of the last century a series of very interesting experiments designed to demonstrate the effects produced upon a sensitive subject by the touch of precious stones and minerals, were made in the case of the "Seeress of Prevorst," Frederike Hauffe (b. 1801), a woman believed to possess remarkable clairvoyant powers.[6] When pieces of granite, porphyry, or flint were placed in her hand, she was not affected in any way. The finest qualities of fluorspar, on the other hand, had a marked action, relaxing the muscles, causing diarrhœa, and producing a sour taste in the mouth; occasionally a somnambulistic state was induced. This latter condition was also produced by Iceland spar and by the sapphire. While the substances so far noted depressed the vital energy, sulphate of barium stimulated the muscles, produced an agreeable warmth of the body, and made the subject feel as though she could fly through the air. If the application of this material was long continued, the pleasurable sensation found expression in laughter. In the case of witherite, a carbonate of barium,

---

[6] Görres, " Die christliche Mystik," Regensburg, 1840, vol. iii, pp. 190 sqq.

this effect was produced to an even greater degree, for if water in which this mineral had been dipped were swallowed, spasms of laughter resulted.

Rock-crystal also was found to possess a strongly stimulating influence, for if put in the hand, it aroused the subject from a half-slumber, and if placed on the pit of the stomach, it had the power to awaken the seeress from a somnambulistic trance, while at the same time an aromatic odor was diffused around. When, however, the application was continued for some time, the muscles stiffened, until finally an epileptic state ensued. Indeed, the rigidity produced was so great that the limbs resisted all attempts to bend them. The same effect, but in a much less degree, was caused by glass, even by looking at it, or by the tones emitted by a glass object when struck. All colorless silicates, the diamond, and even gypsum, had a similar effect, as did also heliotrope and basalt, either of which caused a bitter taste in the mouth.

The most powerful action was that exerted by hematite, the oxide of iron in this substance inducing a kind of paralysis, with a sensation of inner chill; this condition could only be relieved by the application of a piece of witherite. Octahedrons of magnetite (loadstone) caused a sensation of heaviness and convulsive movements of the limbs, even when the material, wrapped up in paper, was brought near the subject. Spinel, in whose composition oxide of chromium enters, caused the same symptoms as loadstone, except that in this case the force seemed to exert itself from the hand upward along the arm, while with the loadstone the action was downward along the arm to the hand, owing to the attractive quality of this magnetic iron. Ruby called forth a sensation of coldness in the tongue, and rendered this member so heavy that only incoherent sounds could be emitted;

the fingers and toes also became cold, and the body was
agitated by a violent shivering; but to all these bad symptoms succeeded a sense of elasticity and well-being, not,
however, without a vague fear that the stone might cause
a renewal of the physical depression. When chrysoprase
was used, chills and shivering resulted, beginning at the
breast and spreading thence over the whole body.

We have touched upon the hypnotic influence exercised by gems, but there can be no doubt that the subject
has not been as carefully studied as it deserves to be.
That the hypnotic state can be induced by gazing fixedly
upon a bright object held just above the eyes is a well-
known fact, but quite probably a similar though not so
pronounced effect results from gazing on a bright object
just before the gazer's eyes. In the case of colored
precious stones, the effects of the various color-rays combine with the light effects and strengthen the impression
upon the optic nerve. All this, however, concerns only
the purely physical impression, but we know that very
often the hypnotic state is produced by a mental impression, by the belief, or the fear, that the state will super-
vene. With precious stones as hypnotizing agents, the
mental impression is widely different, for here the physical impression is heightened by the consciousness of the
value and rarity of the material. The fascination that a
fine set of jewels, with all their sparkle and color, exercises upon the mind of a woman who sees them in their
glorious radiance on the neck, the arms, and the head of
another woman, is not only due to the beauty of the
spectacle, but is largely owing to the consciousness that
they are rare and valuable objects and are perhaps
eloquent witnesses of the power of love. A dash of envy
sometimes serves to render the emotion more complex.

The names of precious stones and semi-precious

stones are frequently used as adjectives, and when so employed convey something more to the mind than do the corresponding adjectives of color. We may instance the following expressions: the "Emerald Isle" and "emerald meadows"; "sapphire seas" and "sapphire eyes"; "ruby wine," "ruby lips," and, in Shakespeare, "the natural ruby of your cheeks"; "coral lips" and "coral ears"; "pearly teeth" and "pearly skin"; "turquoise skies"; "amethystine locks" and, in Roman times, "amber hair." In all these cases the name of the precious mineral is really used as a superlative of the adjective, suggesting the choicest variety of the color or shade. The phrases "hard as adamant" and "clear as crystal" show a similar use of the name of a precious or ornamental stone to express the highest grade of a given quality.

Before the introduction of the "point" system in typography three of the grades of type bore the names of precious stones,—namely, "diamond type," "agate type," and "emerald type"; this latter designation is employed only in England, where "agate type" is called "ruby type." Another size was denominated "pearl type."

A fanciful tale written not long ago treats of the practical inconveniences which would result, could such metaphorical expressions find a realization in fact.[7] At the birth-feast of a certain princess, one of the fairies was not invited; she, nevertheless, made her appearance. After the other fairies had endowed the child with many good qualities, the neglected fairy said, "I will give her vanity, and her vanity shall change her beauty to the things it is said to resemble." However, a friendly fairy

---

[7] Virna Sheard, "The Jewelled Princess," in Canadian Magazine.

came to the rescue, saying, "I will give her unselfishness, and by it she shall turn her beauty back to what she wishes it to be."

The result can easily be imagined. As the little princess grew up, those who wished to flatter her vanity spoke of her "teeth of pearl," of her "golden hair," of her "coral lips," and of her "sapphire eyes." Upon this her teeth changed to pearls, her hair to spun gold, her lips to coral, and her eyes to two magnificent sapphires. However, beautiful as these were, they did not grant the power of sight, so that the unhappy princess became blind. Not long after this a revolution deprived the king and queen of their throne and they were reduced to great poverty. In these straits the daughter sacrificed her "gold-hair" to relieve their wants, and immediately the spell was dissolved and she regained all her natural beauty.

Shelley, who saw the world illumined by the rainbow hues of poetic fancy, wrote of "diamond eyes," "an emerald sky," "the emerald heaven of trees," "the sapphire ocean," "sapphire-tinted skies," "the sapphire floods of interstellar air," and "the chrysolite of sunrise." For some reason, he does not use the ruby, a favorite stone with many poets, and psychologists might find in this a proof that red appeals less strongly to the idealist than do the other colors.

The principal literary sources for the talismanic and therapeutic virtues attributed to ornamental stones may be divided into several groups, at first more or less independent of each other, but combined to a greater or lesser extent by later writers. Pliny gives, sometimes rather grudgingly, a number of superstitions current in his time, but the Alexandrian literature of the second, third, and fourth Christian centuries provides a much richer field for these superstitions, as shown in the Orphic poem "Lithica," the "Cyrianides," attributed to Hermes Trismegistus, the little treatise "On Rivers," which bore the name of Plutarch, and last, but not least, in the work by Damigeron, which purported to be written by an Arab king named Evax, and sent by him to Tiberius or Nero. The influence exerted by the legends surrounding the stones of the high priest's breastplate, and those chosen as foundation stones for the New Jerusalem, will be treated of elsewhere.

In the seventh, eighth, and ninth centuries, a new literature on this subject made its appearance, probably in Asia Minor. Some of the works were originally written in Syriac and later translated into Arabic. Others were composed in the latter language. This source was drawn upon for the production of the Lapidarium of Alfonso X, of Castile. This compilation, although dating in its present Spanish form from the thirteenth century, is based upon a much older original in "Chaldee" (Syriac?). There can be little doubt that many Hindu superstitions, no longer preserved for us in the literature of India, are reproduced in these Syrio-Arabic works, wherein we have also much that is of Alexandrian origin. This indeed is easily explained by history, for the Arabs, through their widely extended conquests, were led to absorb and amalgamate the date they secured, directly or indirectly, from the East and the West.

While this literature was developing in the Mohammedan world, the tradition of Pliny and Solinus was transmitted to the Christian world of the seventh and succeeding centuries by Isidorus of Seville. This brings us to the remarkable poetical treatise on the virtues of precious stones by Marbodus, Bishop of Rennes, a work written at the end of the eleventh century, and often quoted as that of Evax; indeed, it purports to be by him and really contains a good part of the material composing the treatise of Damigeron or Evax. At the same time Marbodus drew freely upon Pliny, either directly or through Isidorus. For the Middle Ages this poem of Marbodus, already translated into Old French in the twelfth century, became known as the "Lapidario" *par excellence,* and furnished a great part of their material to medieval authors on this subject. Soon, however, extracts from the Arabic sources became available, and the whole mass of heterogeneous material was worked over and recombined in a variety of ways.

MARBO=

DEI GALLI POETAE VE
tuſtiſſimi de lapidibus pretioſis Encheri=
dion, cum ſcholijs Pictorij Vil=
lingenſis.

EIVSDEM PICTORII DE
lapide molari carmen.

Lectori.
Qui cupis emunctim gemmarum ſcire medullas,
Huc ueniàs, totum continet iſte liber:
Qui decies ſenis ea pictellis nomina dicit,
Et ſpecies, patriàs, quid ualeàn ſimul.

ANNO M. D.
XXXI.

Title page of the first edition of the poetical treatise on precious stones by Marbodus, Bishop of Rennes, printed in Friburg, 1531.

This complex origin of the traditions explains their almost incomprehensible contradictions regarding the virtues assigned to the different stones, and also the fact that the qualities of one stone are frequently attributed to another one, so that, in the later works on this subject, it becomes quite impossible to present a satisfactory view of the distinguishing qualities and virtues of the separate stones. The habit of copying, without discrimination or criticism, whatever came to hand, and the aim to utilize as much of the borrowed material as possible, is scarcely less a characteristic of the seventeenth and eighteenth century writers than it is of those of a later date. This is in part an excusable and even an unavoidable defect, but it should be minimized as much as possible.

The treatise known under the title "Cyrianides" was, as we have noted, a product of the Alexandrian school. It was asserted to be the work of Hermes Trismegistus, the name given by the Greeks to the Egyptian god Thoth.

Here we have a specimen of the species of magic known as litteromancy, or divination by means of the letters of the alphabet, since a stone, a bird, a plant, and a fish, each beginning with the same letter and signifying the four elements, are given for each of the twenty-four letters of the Greek alphabet. These four objects were to be grouped together to form a talisman, the bird being usually engraved on the stone, while a portion of the fish and of the plant was placed in the bezel of the ring in which the stone was to be set.[8] Another, almost contemporary work, is the exceedingly curious and interesting treatise by St. Epiphanius, Bishop of Constantia, on the twelve gems on the " Breastplate of Judgment" of the high priest (Ex., xxviii, 15–21). This unique production is in the form of a letter addressed to Diodorus, Bishop of Tyre, and it is peculiarly valuable as the

S A N C T I

PATRIS E*PIPHANII EPI*SCOPI CYPRI. AD DIOdorum Tyri epiſcopum, De XI I, Gemmis,quæ erant in veſte Aaronis, Liber Græcus, & è regione Latinus, Iola Hierotárantino interprete: cum Corollano Conradi Geſneri.

TIGVRI M.D. LXVI.

Title page of the first edition of the Greek treatise by St. Epiphanius on the Gems of the Breastplate, with a Latin version. Edited and issued at Zürich in 1566 (1565) by Conrad Gesner.

---

[8] De Mély, " Les lapidaires de l'antiquité et du moyen-âge," vol. ii, "Les lapidaires grecs," Paris, 1898, pp. 1–50.

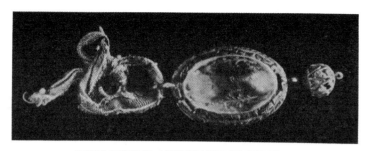

ROCK-CRYSTAL AMULET SET IN SILVER.
Bohemian, tenth century. Field Museum of Natural History.

ROCK-CRYSTAL PLACQUE, ANCIENT MEXICAN.
Field Museum Collection, Chicago.

first of a long series of attempts to elucidate the question as to the identity of the twelve stones. The special virtues of each stone are also given, and this treatise may be regarded as the prototype of all the Christian writings on the symbolism of stones.

A most interesting medieval treatise on the virtues of precious stones forms part of the *De rerum natura* of Thomas de Cantimpré (1201–1270), who was a pupil of Albertus Magnus and composed his work between 1230 and 1244. The Latin text has never been printed, but the book was translated into German by Konrad von Megenberg about 1350. Strange to say, the translator did not know the name of the writer and supposed when he began to translate the book that it was by Albertus Magnus. In many cases Thomas de Cantimpré merely copies the statements of older authors, but occasionally he gives us new material, or at least a new version of his originals.

THI
HISTORY
O.F
Jewels,
And of the Principal Riches of the *EAST* and *WEST*.
Taken from
The Relation of Divers of the Moft Famous Travellers of
OUR AGE.
Attended with
FAIR DISCOVERIES,
Conducing to the knowledge of the
UNIVERSE and *TRADE.*

LONDON,
Printed by *T. N.* for *Hubert Kemp,* at the Sign of the Ship in the *Upper Walk* of the *New Exchange.* 1671.

Title page of one of the earliest treatises on precious stones published in England.

The renowned medieval philosopher and theologian, Albertus Magnus (1193–1280), for a short time Bishop of Ratisbon, and who later taught theology in the University of Paris and had the great St. Thomas Aquinas for a pupil, was not altogether free from the superstitious notions of his time, traces of which appear in certain of his numerous writings. Many years after his death some of this material was extracted from his works and, amplified by additions from other sources, was published under the title "Secrets des vertus des Herbes, Pierres et Bestes.'' Of this there are two versions, one being an epitome of the other and termed respectively ''Le Grand Albert'' and ''Le Petit Albert.'' These little books were often reprinted and widely circulated, and eventually enjoyed great popularity among the French peasants. Indeed, even to the present day they may still be met with in out-of-the-way parts of rural France.

Among literary deceptions one of the boldest was that practised in the early part of the seventeenth century by Ludovico Dolce. This writer made, in 1565, a literal translation into Italian of the ''Speculum lapidum'' of Camillo Leonardo, printed in Venice in 1502, and he had the courage to issue it as his own work, under the title ''Trattato delle gemme chè produce la natura.'' In view of the general familiarity with Latin among the better classes at that period, and the numerous fine libraries existing in Venice at the time, it seems most extraordinary that Dolce should have been successful in palming off this work as his own, but even to-day citations are made from Dolce's ''Trattato delle gemme'' and from Leonardo's ''Speculum lapidum,'' as though these were distinct works.

II

On the Use of Precious and Semi-Precious Stones as Talismans and Amulets

THE use of precious stones in early times as amulets and talismans is shown in many ancient records, and several scholars have assumed that the belief in the magic efficacy of stones gave rise to their use as objects of personal adornment. It is, of course, very difficult either to prove or to disprove such a theory, for, even in the case of the oldest texts, we must bear in mind that they do not in the least represent primitive conditions, and that many thousands of years must have elapsed before a people could attain the grade of civilization necessary for the production of even the simplest literature. For this reason, certain investigators have preferred to seek for a solution of this problem in the customs and habits of the so-called uncivilized peoples of our own time; but we must not forget that conditions which seem to us very rudimentary are, nevertheless, the result of a long process of development. Even if this development was arrested many centuries or millenniums ago, it must have required a very considerable period of time to evolve such usages and conventions as are found even among the lowest races. Indeed, many uncivilized peoples have very complicated rules and observances, testifying to considerable thought and reflection.

Fetichism in all its forms depends upon an imperfect conception of what constitutes life and conscious being, so that will and thought are attributed to inanimate objects. We can observe this in the case of animals and very young children, who regard any moving object as endowed with life. In the case of stones, however, it seems probable that those supposed to be the abode of spirits, good or evil, were selected because their natural form suggested that of some animal or of some portion of the human body. On the other hand, the wearing of what we call precious stones is more likely to have been due to the attraction exercised by bright colors upon the eye of the beholder and to the desire to display some distinguishing mark that would command attention and admiration for the wearer. This tendency runs through the higher animal kingdom, and its workings have served as a foundation for the theory of natural selection.

It seems likely that we have here the true explanation of the motive for the gathering, preserving, and wearing of precious stones. Since these objects are motionless, they can scarcely have impressed the mind of primitive man with the idea that they were alive; they were not imposing by their mass, as were large stones, and their crystalline form scarcely figured any known living shape. Hence their chief, we may even say their only attraction was their color and brilliancy. What effect these qualities had upon the visual sense of primitive man may be safely inferred from the effect such objects produce upon infants. The baby has no fear in regard to a small and brilliantly colored object which is shown to it, but will eagerly put out its hand to seize, hold, and gaze upon a bright-colored stone. As the object is quite passive and easily handled, there is nothing to suggest any lurking power to harm, and therefore there is nothing to interfere with the pleasurable sensation aroused in the optic nerve by the play of color. In this naïve admiration of what is brilliant and colored, the infant undoubtedly represents for us the mental attitude of primitive man.

Probably the first objects chosen for personal adornment were those easily strung or bound together,—for instance, certain perforated shells and brilliant seeds; the softer stones, wherein holes could be easily bored by the help of the simplest tools, probably came next, while the harder gems must have been hoarded as pretty toys long before they could be adjusted for use as ornaments.

Unquestionably, when these objects had once been worn, there was a disposition to attribute certain happenings to their influence and power, and in this way there arose a belief in their efficacy, and, finally, the conviction that they were the abodes of powerful spirits. In this, as in many other things, man's first and instinctive appreciation was the truest, and it has required centuries of enlightenment to bring us back to this love of precious stones for their esthetic beauty alone. Indeed, even to-day, we can see the power of superstitious belief in the case of the opal, which some timid people still fear to wear, although until three or four centuries ago this stone was thought to combine all the virtues of the various colored gems, the hues of which are united in its sparkling light.

A proof that bright and colored objects were attractive in themselves, and were first gathered up and preserved by primitive man for this reason alone, may be found in the fact that certain birds, notable the *Chlamydera* of Australia, related to our ravens, after constructing for themselves pretty arbors, strew the floors with variegated pebbles, so arranged as to suggest a mosaic pavement. At the entrance of the arbors are heaped up pieces of bone, shells, feathers, and stones, which have often been brought from a considerable distance, this giving evidence that the birds have not selected these objects at random. It is strange that the attraction exercised upon the sense of sight by anything brilliant and colored, which is at the same time easily portable and can be handled or worn, should be overlooked by those who are disposed to assert that all ornaments of this kind were originally selected and preserved solely or principally because of their supposed talismanic qualities.

The theory that colored and brilliant stones were first collected by men because of their beauty rather than because of their talismanic virtues, is corroborated by the statement made that seals select with considerable care the stones they swallow, and observers on the fishing grounds have noted this and believe that pebbles of chalcedony and serpentine found there have been brought by the seals.[1]

The popular derivation of the word "amulet" from an Arabic word *hamalât*, signifying something suspended or worn, is not accepted by the best Arabic scholars, and it seems probable that the name is of Latin origin, in spite of the fact that no very satisfactory etymology can be given. Pliny's use of *amuletum* shows that with him the word did not always denote an object that was worn on the person, although this later became its meaning. The old etymology given by Varro (118–29 B.C.), who derived *amuletum* from the verb *amoliri*, "to remove," "to drive away," may not be quite in accord with modern philology, but still has something to recommend it as far as the sense goes, for the amulet was certainly believed to hold dangers aloof, or even to remove them. Talis-

---

[1] Lucas, " The Swallowing Stones by Seals," Science, N. S., vol. xx, No. 512, pp. 537, 538; Report of Fur Seal Investigation, vol. iii, p. 68.

1. Necklace of rock-crystal and amethyst beads, transparent and translucent; very pale; from Egypt. First century.
2. Necklace of antique emeralds with gold beads and amazon stones; from Egypt. First century A.D.

man, however, a word not used in classical times, undoubtedly comes from the Arabic *tilsam,* this being in turn derived from τέλεσμα, used in late Greek to signify an initiation, or an incantation.

It has been remarked that in the earliest Stone Age there is no trace of either idols or images; the art of this period being entirely profane. In the later Stone Age, however, entirely different ideas seem to have gained the ascendancy, for a majority of the objects of plastic art so far discovered have a religious significance. This has evidently proceeded from the conception that every image of a living object absorbs something of the essence of the object itself, and this conception, while a primitive one, still presupposes a certain degree of development. This rule applies more especially to amulets, which were therefore fashioned as beautifully as primitive art permitted, that they might become fitting abodes for the benevolent spirits believed to animate them and render them efficacious.[2]

A curious idol or talisman from Houaïlou, New Caledonia, is in the collection of Signor Giglioli. This is a stone bearing naturally a rude resemblance to the human form.[3] We can easily understand that such an object was looked upon as the abode of some spirit, for similar strange natural formations have been regarded with a species of superstitious awe by peoples much more civilized than the natives of New Caledonia.

For the Middle Ages and even down to the seventeenth century, the talismanic virtues of precious stones were believed in by high and low, by princes and peas-

---

[2] Hoernes, " Urgeschichte der bildenden Kunst," Wien, 1898, p. 108.

[3] Giglioli, " Materiale per lo studio della ' Età della Pietra,' " Archivio per l'Antropologia e l'Etnologia, vol. xxxi, p. 83, Firenze, 1901.

ants, by the learned as well as by the ignorant. Here and there, however, a note of scepticism was sometimes apparent, as in the famous reply of the court jester of Emperor Charles V, to the question, ''What is the property of the turquoise?'' ''Why,'' replied he, ''if you should happen to fall from a high tower whilst you were wearing a turquoise on your finger, the turquoise would remain unbroken.''

The doctrine of sympathy and antipathy found expression in the belief that the very substance of certain stones was liable to modification by the condition of health or even by the thoughts of the wearer. In case of sickness or approaching death the lustre of the stones was dimmed, or else their bright colors were darkened, and unfaithfulness or perjury produced similar phenomena. Concerning the turquoise, the prosaic explanation can be offered that this stone is affected to a certain extent by the secretions of the skin; but popular superstition saw the same phenomena in the ruby, the diamond, and other stones not possessing the sensitiveness of the turquoise. Hence the true explanation is to be found in the prevailing idea that an occult sympathy existed between stone and wearer. The sentiment underlying the conception is well expressed by Emerson in the following lines from ''The Amulet'':

> Give me an amulet
>   That keeps intelligence with you,—
> Red when you love, and rosier red,
>   And when you love not, pale and blue.

A Persian legend of the origin of diamonds and precious stones shows that in the East these beautiful objects were looked upon as the source of much sin and sorrow. We are told that when God created the world he made no useless things, such as gold, silver, precious stones, and diamonds; but Satan, who is always eager to bring evil among men, kept a close watch to spy out the appetites and passions of the human mind. To his great satisfaction he noted that Eve passionately loved the many-colored flowers that decked the Garden of Eden; he therefore undertook to imitate their brightness and color out of earth, and in this way were produced colored precious stones and diamonds. These in after time so strongly appealed to the greed and covetousness of mankind that they have been the cause of much crime and wretchedness.[4]

The present age could afford us nearly as many examples of faith in talismans and amulets as any epoch in the past, if people were willing to confess their real beliefs. However, they are half-ashamed of their fondness for such objects, and fail to see that, back of all the folly and superstition that may find expression in this way, there is a deeper meaning in these talismans than we at first perceive. We may be disposed to smile when we are told that many of the soldiers in the Austro-Prussian War of 1866 carried amulets of some kind upon their persons, and that the great Marshal Canrobert trusted to the protection of an amulet in the Crimean campaign. Of course the Russian army, during the Russo-Japanese War, was amply provided with amulets, religious medals or pictures to which a special virtue had been given by a priestly blessing.

In all these cases, however, it is not the object itself, but the idea for which it stands and which it incorporates, that gives confidence to the wearer, and in this sense the wearing of a talisman is no more a proof of blind super-

---

[4] Rose, "Handleiding tot de Kennis van diamanten," etc., Amsterdam, 1891, p. 110.

stition than is the devotion to a flag, in itself only a few square feet of silk or bunting, but, nevertheless, the symbol of the noblest ideas and feelings, of patriotic devotion to one's native land and to one's fellow-countrymen. The tendency to give a substantial visible form to an abstract idea is so deeply rooted in humanity that it must be looked upon as responding to a human necessity. It is only very rarely that purely intellectual conceptions can satisfy us; they must be given some external, palpable and visible form to exert their greater influences.

Although it may bear a certain superficial likeness to fetichism, this use of signs and symbols is something entirely and radically different, for the idea is never lost sight of, it is only strengthened and vivified by the contemplation of the symbol. Hence, while we know quite well that the symbol is nothing in itself, we know just as well that it has a real power in its relation to the idea it typifies, and we can no more be indifferent to its injury or destruction than we could be indifferent to the injury or destruction of a cherished memento of one whom we have loved and lost.

What super-subtle sense is it that enables some women to endow their gems with a certain individuality, and leads them to feel that these cold, inanimate objects partake of human emotion? A French writer, Mme. Catulle Mendès, gives expression to this when she says that she always wears as many of her rings as possible, because her gems feel slighted when she leaves them unworn. She continues:

I have a ruby which grows dull, two turquoises which become pale as death, aquamarines which look like siren's eyes filled with tears, when I forget them too long. How sad I should feel if precious stones did not love to rest upon me!

MOSAICS OF TURQUOISE AND ENAMELLED CARNELIAN BEADS,
FROM THIBET.

Field Museum, Chicago.

A very beautiful and curious object was found in the Australian opal-fields in 1909. This is a reptilean skeleton resembling a small serpent that has become opalized by natural processes. Perfect in all its details, which are rendered more striking by the splendid play of color, this specimen of Nature's handiwork possesses a beauty and an interest exceeding those to be found in any work of man. As an amulet it certainly is *sui generis,* and in ancient times would have been valued at an immense sum, for the figure of a serpent was a favorite symbol of medical science; even to-day there is little doubt that this strange object will be eagerly sought for by collectors, and will appeal more especially to all who are interested in occult science, and to all who appreciate the poetic and perhaps mystic significance of form, sign, and symbol.

It is impossible to over-estimate the effect of color in determining the supposed influence of gems upon the fortunes or health of the wearers. When we gaze upon the beautiful play of light emitted by a fine ruby or sapphire, we are all conscious of the æsthetic effect produced; but in earlier times, when scientific ideas were not yet prevalent, many other considerations combined to give a peculiar significance to these brilliant gems. Rare and costly as they were, they were supposed to possess mystic and occult powers and were thought to be the abode of spirits, sometimes benevolent and sometimes malevolent, but always endowed with the power to influence human destinies for weal or woe. Coupled with this was the instinctive appreciation of the essential qualities of certain rays of light, and modern science, far from doing away with these ideas, has rather seemed to find a good reason for them. We all know the therapeutic value of the ultra-violet rays, and when the uninstructed mind saw therein the embodiment of purity and chastity, it perhaps realized this health-giving and beneficent function. In the same way the idea of passion was associated with the red and radiant ruby, another concept the relative truth of which has been demonstrated by spectrum analysis, since the red rays are heat-giving and vivifying. But this was not the only source of these primitive ideas in regard to color; the therapeutic effect was often sought and found in some fancied analogy between the color of the gem and the character of the malady or infirmity to be cured. Thus, yellow stones were supposed to be especially efficacious in cases of jaundice, an instance of instinctive homœopathy, based on the dictum *similia similibus curantur.* Following out this train of thought, the red stones were endowed with the power of checking the flow of blood; especially the so-called bloodstone was prescribed for this use, and it was supposed that by its mere touch it could stop the most violent hemorrhages. Green was regarded as the color most beneficial for the sight, and to the emerald and other green stones was ascribed great curative power in this respect. Here, however, the simple influence of the color was later combined with its symbolical significance. In heathen mythology this showed itself in the ascription of the emerald to Venus, as the exponent of the reproductive energies of nature, while in the Christian conception these stones became typical of the resurrection, of the birth into a new and purer life. Nowhere can we find a better illustration of the transforming effect of distinct and diametrically opposite concepts upon the impressions made by natural objects. The pure and colorless and yet brilliant stones, such as the diamond and all other white stones, were naturally brought into connection with the moon, although the diamond, because of its superior qualities and exceptional brilliance and value, was frequently looked upon as the gem of the sun. All gems associated with the moon partook of its enigmatic character. Illuminating the witching hour of the night, when malevolent and treacherous spirits were supposed to hold sway, the moon was sometimes regarded as baleful, as may be seen in the idea that associated lunacy with exposure to the bright rays of the moon; at other times it was supposed to have the power to conjure these evil influences and to drive off the powers of darkness.

The symbolical significance of the colors of precious stones is treated at considerable length by Giacinto Gimma,[5] who has gathered together a great quantity of material on the subject.

Yellow worn by a man denoted secrecy, and was appropriate for the silent lover; worn by a woman it indicated generosity. Golden yellow was, of course, the symbol of the sun and of Sunday. The precious stone was the chrysolite or the yellow jacinth. The animal connected with the color was the lion, doubtless from the association of the zodiacal sign Leo with the midsummer sun. Of the seven ages of man yellow typified adolescence. Roman matrons covered their heads with a yellow veil to show their hope of offspring and happiness. Because garments of this color were a sign of grandeur and nobility, a golden vestment is assigned to the Queen of Heaven as a sign of her pre-eminence, as we read in Psalm xlv, 9: "Upon thy right hand did stand the queen in gold of Ophir." Gimma's explanation of

---

[5] "Della storia naturale delle Gemme," Napoli, 1730, Vol. I, pp. 131–137.

this as referring to the Virgin Mary is in accord with the Catholic exegesis of his time.

White signified for men friendship, religion, integrity; for women, contemplation, affability, and purity. It was associated with the moon and with Monday and was represented by the pearl. The animal having an affinity with white was quite naturally the ermine. The mystic number was seven, and white was the color of infancy. Among the ancients white was a sign of mourning and sadness, and the Greek matrons attired themselves in white on the death of their husbands. Gimma states that in his time, in Rome, widows used to wear white as mourning for their husbands, while throughout Italy a white band worn around the head was a sign of widowhood.

Red garments on a man indicated command, nobility, lordship, and vengeance; on a woman, pride, obstinacy, and haughtiness. This was the color of the planet Mars and of Tuesday; it was represented by the ruby. Why the lynx should have been selected as the animal for red is rather difficult to understand, but, as the most vivid color, the choice of red as a type of full manhood need not surprise us. Its number was the potent nine, three multiplied by itself. The ancients covered with a red cloth the biers of those who had died valiantly in battle, as Homer [6] shows when he relates that the brothers and companions of Hector covered the urn containing the hero's ashes with soft purple (scarlet) robes. Plutarch asserts that the Lacedemonians clothed their soldiers in red to strike terror into the hearts of their enemies and to manifest a thirst for blood. We might perhaps say much the same of the English "red-coats" to-day. The

---

[6] Il., xxiv, 795, 796.

Italian code of criminal laws known as the "Digesto Nuovo" was bound in red, to signify that a bloody death awaited thieves and murderers.

Blue on a man's dress indicated wisdom and high and magnanimous thoughts; on a woman's dress, jealousy in love, politeness, and vigilance. Friday and Venus were represented by blue, and the celestial-hued sapphire was the stone in which this color appeared in all its beauty. Blue was a fit symbol of the age of childhood, but it is less easy to understand the choice of the goat as the animal associated with the color. The significant number was six. Natural science, the contemplation of the heavens and of the heavenly bodies, and the study of stellar influences were all typified by blue.

Green signified for men joyousness, transitory hope, and the decline of friendship; for women, unfounded ambition, childish delight, and change. The early verdure of spring might be regarded as at once a symbol of hope and of eventual disappointment, for it must soon pass away. Mercury, and Wednesday, the day of Mercury, were both typified by green, the sly fox being selected as the animal is sympathy with the wily god. The typical green stone is the emerald, youth is the age of man represented by the color, and five the magic number expressing it. In ancient times green was used in the case of those who died in the flower of youth, an emerald being sometimes placed on the index-finger of the corpse, as a sign that the light of hope was spent, for the lower part of the torches used in religious ceremonies was marked with green. Fulvius Pellegrinus relates that, in the tomb of Tullia, the dearly-beloved daughter of Cicero, there was found an emerald, the most beautiful that had ever been seen. This passed into the hands of the Marchesana di Mantova, Isabella Gonzaga da Este. In Italy the graves of young virgins and of children were covered with green branches. When the Codex Justinianus was rediscovered and added to the other Pandects, it was bound in green to signify that these laws were rejuvenated.

Black for men means gravity, good sense, constancy, and fortitude; for young women, fickleness and foolishness, but for married women, constant love and perseverance. The planet Saturn and Saturday are denoted by black. Strange to say, the diamond, the white gem *par excellence,* was selected to represent this sombre hue. Perhaps to offset this the animal chosen was the hog. As black was a mourning color, we need not be surprised that it typified decrepitude. The number eight, the double square, was supposed to have some affinity with black. Black is a symbol of envy, for the thoughts which aim at another's injury cloud the soul and afflict the body. The book of laws treating of dispositions made in view of death was bound in black. The sinister significance of black is well illustrated by what is told of the ruthless Tartar Tamerlane. When he attacked a city, he caused a white tent to be pitched for himself on the first day of the siege, as a sign that mercy would be shown to the inhabitants if they immediately surrendered; on the second day a red tent was substituted, signifying that if the city yielded, all the leaders would be put to death; on the third day, however, a black tent was raised, an ominous signal that no mercy would be shown and that all the inhabitants would be slaughtered.

Violet for a man denoted sober judgment, industry, and gravity; for a woman, high thoughts and religious love. It was the color of the planet Jupiter and of Thursday. As with blue, the sapphire was conceived to present violet most attractively. That the bull should be selected as the animal represented by this color probably arose from some mythological connection with Jupiter, possibly the myth of Europa and the bull. Violet was the color of old age and was associated with the number three.

The influence of color upon the nerves has been noted by some of the leading authorities on hypnotism. For example, Dr. Paul Ferez, finding that red light is stimulating and blue-violet calming, suggests that those who treat patients by means of hypnotism should have two rooms for their reception. In one of these rooms the curtains, wall-paper, chair-coverings, etc., would be red, while in the other they would be of a violet-blue hue. Those suffering from a lack of will-power or from lassitude and depression are to be received in the red room, and those who are a prey to over-excitability are introduced into the blue room. Moreover, according to Dr. Ferez, the sedative qualities of the violet-blue can be utilized in inducing the hypnotic state. For this purpose he recommends a violet-blue disk, which is to be rotated rapidly before the eyes of the patient, the movement serving to attract and hold his gaze better than any immovable object would do.[7]

Red stones such as rubies, carbuncles, and garnets, whose color suggested that of blood, were not only believed to confer invulnerability from wounds, but some Asiatic tribes have used garnets as bullets, upon the contrary principle that this blood-colored stone would inflict a more deadly wound than would a leaden bullet. Such bullets were used by the rebellious Hanzas, in

[7] Paper by Dr. Paul Ferez in the Revue de l'Hypnotisme, Paris, No. 10, April, 1906, p. 306.

3

1892, during their hostilities with the British troops on the Kashmir frontier, and many of these precious missiles were preserved as curiosities.

In his "Colloquy on Pilgrimages," Erasmus makes one of the speakers ask, "Dost thou not see how the artificer Nature delights to represent all things by colors and forms, but more especially in gems?" He then proceeds to enumerate the various images of natural objects in stones. In the ceraunia appeared the thunder-bolt; in the pyrope, living fire; the chalazia (rock-crystal) preserved the form and coldness of the hailstone even if cast into the fire. In the emerald were shown the deep and translucent waves of the sea; the carcinia imitated the form of crabs; the echites, of vipers; the hieracites, of hawks; the geranites, of cranes. The ætites offered the image of an eagle with a white tail; the taos had the form of a peacock; the chelonites, of an asp; while the myrmecites bore within the figure of an ant.[8] The stones bearing this latter name were probably specimens of amber containing ants.

The Greek names of these stones enumerated by Erasmus signify their real or supposed resemblance to certain natural objects, or to something characteristic of such objects. Many of them were fossils, preserving the form of some living organism; a few were entirely fabulous; still others owed their names to some legend or myth illustrating their fancied therapeutic virtues, as in the case of the ætites (eagle-stone) said to be found in the eagle's nest. Evidently this was a quartz pebble.

The oldest magic formulas that have been preserved for us are those of the Sumerians, the founders of the

[8] Erasmi, " Colloquia," Lipsiæ, 1713, pp. 597–8. Suggested by Pliny, lib. xxxvii, cap. 71–73.

ancient civilization of Babylonia. Some of them contain references to the use of precious stones as amulets, as appears in the following specimen:

> Cords of light-colored wool,
> Offered (?) with a pure hand,
> For jaundice of the eye,
> Bind on the right side (of the patient).
> A lululti ring, with sparkling stones
> Brought from his own land,
> For inflammation of the eye,
> On the little finger
> Of his left (hand), place.[*]

A curious Babylonian mythological text represents the solar diety Ninib, the son of Bel, as determining the fate of various stones by pronouncing a blessing or a curse upon them. For instance, the dolomite was blessed and declared to be fit material for the statues of kings, while a substance called the *elu* stone was cursed, proclaimed to be unfit for working, and doomed to disintegration. Alabaster was favored by the god, but chalcedony aroused his anger and was condemned.[10]

In these Sumero-Assyrian inscriptions, there is also mention of two stones, the *aban râme* and the *aban la râme*, the "Stone of Love" and the "Stone of Hate" (lit. "non-love").[11] Evidently these stones were believed to excite one or other of these contradictory passions in the hearts of the wearers, and they may be compared with the stones of memory and forgetfulness in the "Gesta Romanorum."

In an ancient Egyptian burial-place at Shêch Abd el-

---

[*] Morris Jastrow, "Die Religion Babyloniens und Assyriens," vol. i, Giessen, 1905, p. 374.

[10] Morris Jastrow, l. c., p. 462.

[11] Delitzsch, "Assyrisches Wörterbuch," Leipzig, 1896, p. 604.

Qurna, excavated by Passalaqua, was found the mummy of a young woman. Not only was it evident from the rich ornaments adorning the body that she had been of noble birth, but it was also apparent that she must have been exceedingly beautiful in form and feature, and must have died in the flower of her age. The hair was artistically braided and adorned with twenty bronze hairpins. About her neck was a remarkably beautiful necklace composed of four rows of beads with numerous pendants representing divinities and sacred symbols. There were also two smaller necklaces with beads of gold, lapis-lazuli, and carnelian; two large jewelled earrings hung from her ears, and on the index-finger of her right hand was a ring set with a scarab; a gold belt garnished with lapis-lazuli and carnelians was bound about her waist and a gold bracelet adorned with semiprecious stones encircled her left wrist. In the sarcophagus was a beautiful mirror of golden-yellow bronze, and three alabaster vases, one still containing some balm or perfume, and another some galena (native lead sulphide) to be used as a cosmetic for the eyes, as well as a little ebony pencil for its application. All these objects are now in the Egyptian collection of the Berlin Museum, and they probably belong to the period of the XVIII Dynasty, about 1500 B.C.

The principal necklace was undoubtedly regarded by the fair Egyptian as an amulet of great power, but it failed to protect her from an untimely end; perhaps, however, its virtues may have aided her soul in its passage through the trials and tests imposed in the underworld. Of the numerous pendants which lent to the necklace its peculiar quality as an amulet, three, in carnelian, figure the god Bes; seven, also in carnelian, the hippo-

potamus-goddess Toeris, of whom there are besides two
representations in lapis-lazuli; then we have a heart of
lapis-lazuli; a cat of lapis-lazuli; four falcons of carnelian; one crocodile of carnelian and two of lapis-lazuli;
four fish of carnelian, as well as two others of a blackish-
white and of a green stone, respectively, and two scor-
pions of carnelian, and seven flower-forms of the same
stone. The greater part of the beads in this necklace
are of annular form, of gold, electrum, ivory, or lapis-
lazuli; there are a few larger annular or spherical beads
of carnelian, chrysoprase, and malachite, and measuring
up to 3.5 cm. in diameter.[12]

A necklace, from the time of the Old Empire (c. 3500
B.C.), and having for its chief adornment a turquoise
pendant rudely fashioned into the form of an ibex, was
found by the German Orient-Gesellschaft at Abusîr el-
Meleq in 1905. This necklace, the parts of which were
found about the neck of a body, presumably that of a
young man, was composed of rounded and annular beads
of carnelian and shell, as well as of flat, perforated fragments of turquoise and almandine garnet and an ap-
proximately lozenge-shaped bead of amethyst 1.7 cm.
long and 1.4 cm. broad. The chief ornament was the
turquoise ibex 1.7 cm. in length and 0.9 cm. high.[13] This
figure suggests a comparison with the animal and bird
forms fashioned out of turquoise that have been found
in Indian graves in Arizona and New Mexico, and it
probably had the quality of a fetich, or at least of a

---

[12] " Aegyptische Goldschmiedearbeit," ed. by Heinrich Schäffer,
Berlin, 1910, pp. 25–32; necklace figured on Pl. V, other objects on
Pls. V–VII.
    [13] Ibid., p. 14, Pl. II, figs. 3a, 3b.

talisman, intended to guard the wearer of the necklace from harm.

That there was in Egypt a strong inclination to use a certain particular stone for a given amulet, will be noted in the case of those inscribed with special chapters of the Book of the Dead. This is also true of amulets of certain forms. For instance, the head-rest amulet is usually of hematite as is also the carpenter's square. Of the heart amulets, numbering 47 in the rich collections of the Cairo Museum, nine are of carnelian, four of hematite, two of lapis-lazuli, and two each of green porphyry and green jasper, carnelian being thus the most favored among the more precious materials. Amulets of animal form are plentifully represented in this collection, figuring a large variety of members of the animal kingdom such as the hippopotamus, crocodile, lion, bull, cow, hare, dog-headed ape, cat, dog (somewhat doubtful), jackal, hedgehog, frog, hawk, cobra and fishes, to which list may be added a four-headed ram and a ram-headed sphinx.[14]

One of the special uses of amulets was for seafaring people, for, in ancient times especially, all who went down to the sea in ships were greatly in need of protection from the fury of the elements when they embarked in their small sailing-vessels. A fragment of a Greek Lapidary,[15] probably written in the third or fourth century of our era, gives a list of seven amulets peculiarly adapted for this purpose. The number might suggest a connection with the days of the week, and the amulets

---

[14] See Reisner, "Catalogue générale des antiquités égyptiennes du Musée du Caire: Amulets" Le Caire, 1907.

[15] Pitra, "Specilegium Solesmense," Parisiis, 1855, vol. iii, p. 393.

were perhaps regarded as most efficacious when used on the respective days.

In the first were set a carbuncle and a chalcedony; this amulet protected sailors from drowning. The second had for its gem either of two varieties of the adamas,— one, the Macedonian, being likened to ice (this was probably rock-crystal), while the other, the Indian, of a silvery hue, may possibly have been our corundum; however, the Macedonian stone was regarded as the better. The third amulet bore the beryl, "transparent, brilliant, and of a sea-green hue," evidently the aquamarine beryl; this banished fear. The fourth had for its gem the *druops,* "white in the centre," probably the variety of agate so much favored as a protector against the spell of the Evil Eye. A coral was placed in the fifth amulet, and this was to be attached to the prow of the ship with strips of seal-skin; it guarded the vessel from winds and waves in all waters. For the sixth amulet the *ophiokiolus* stone was selected, most probably a kind of banded agate, for it is said to have been girdled with stripes like the body of a snake; whoever wore this had no need to fear the surging ocean. The seventh and last of these nautical amulets bore a stone called *opsianos,* apparently a resinous or bituminous material, possibly a kind of jet; this came from Phrygia and Galatia, and the amulet wherein it was set was a great protection for all who journeyed by sea or by river.

The ancient treatises on the magic art show that the use of amulets was considered to be indispensable for those who dared to evoke the dark spirits of the nether-world, for without the protection afforded by his amulet the magician ran the risk of being attacked by these spirits. One of these texts gives directions for preparing an amulet, or *phylacterion,* for the "undertaking";

for this a "sweet-smelling" loadstone should be chosen, and should be cut heart-shaped and engraved with the figure of Hecate.[16]

A costly Chinese amulet consists of the diamond, the ruby, and the emerald, to which are added the pearl and coral; Oriental sapphire and topaz are classed with the ruby. An amulet containing these five substances is thought to combine the protecting influences of the different deities presiding over them, and is supposed to lengthen the wearer's life. Sometimes these five princely gems are wrapped up in a paper bearing the names of the respective divinities, to which is added the name of the moon, and those of the twenty-seven constellations, or houses of the moon. Such an amulet, suspended at the entrance of a house, is believed to afford protection to the inmates.[17]

In the language of the ancient Mexicans blood was called *chalchiuhatl*, or "water of precious stones," as the quintessence of what were regarded as the most costly things.[18] Although such poetic designations are in modern times mere figures of speech, among primitive peoples they are more significant, and it is highly probable that with the Aztecs, as with other peoples, the wearing of precious stones was believed to enrich the blood and thus to promote health and vigor, for "the blood is the life."

That gems had sex is asserted by the earliest writers

---

[16] Kropatschek, "De amuletorum apud antiquos usu," Gryphiæ, 1907, p. 24 (Paris papyrus, 2630).

[17] Surindro Mohun Tagore, "Mani Málá," Pt. II, Calcutta, 1881, p. 943.

[18] Seler, "Codex Borgia: Eine altmexicanische Bilderschrift," Berlin, 1904, vol. i, p. 16.

as well as by many of those of a later date. While this must usually be understood as a poetic way of indicating a difference in shade, the darker varieties being regarded as male and the lighter ones as female, Theophrastus, the earliest Greek writer on precious stones, clearly shows that this sexual distinction was sometimes seriously made, for he declares that, wonderful as it might seem, certain gems were capable of producing offspring.

This strange idea was still prevalent in the sixteenth century, and ingenious explanations were sometimes given of the cause of this phenomenon, as appears in the following account by Rueus of germinating diamonds: [19]

It has recently been related to me by a lady worthy of credence, that a noblewoman, descended from the illustrious house of Luxemburg, had in her possession two diamonds which she had inherited, and which produced others in such miraculous wise, that whoever examined them at stated intervals judged that they had engendered progeny like themselves. The cause of this (if it be permissible to philosophize regarding such a strange matter) would seem to be that the celestial energy in the parent stones, qualified by some one as " *vis adamantifica*," first changes the surrounding air into water, or some similar substance, and then condenses and hardens this into the diamond gem.

The pearl-fishers of Borneo are said to preserve carefully every ninth pearl they find, and place them in a bottle with two grains of rice for each pearl, believing, in spite of all evidence to the contrary, that these particular pearls have the power to engender and breed others. Custom and superstition require that each bottle shall have the finger of a dead man as a stopper.

Talismanic influences are taken into account in the

---

[19] Francisci Ruei, " De gemmis," Tiguri, 1566, f. 4.

wearing of jewelry by Orientals, two bracelets being
frequently worn lest one member should become jealous
of the other, thus disturbing the equilibrium of the
whole organism. The piercing of the ears for ear-rings
has been attributed to a desire to chastise the ear for
its indiscretion in hearing secrets not intended to be
heard, while costly and ornamental ear-rings are set in
the ears to console those
parts of our anatomy for
the suffering caused by
the operation of piercing.
In the case of necklaces of
brilliant metal, adorned
with pendants of glittering
stones, the talismanic purpose is to attract the beholder's gaze and thus
ward off the mysterious
and dangerous emana-
tions set forth by the Evil
Eye; the necklace, or its
ornaments, are supposed
to perform a similar ser-
vice to that rendered by
the lightning-rod in di-
verting the electric dis-
charge.

Capitulū.lrruiif.

PEARL DEALER.
From the "Hortus Sanitatis" of Johannis
de Cuba [Strassburg, Jean Pryss, ca. 1483]: De
lapidibus, cap. lxxviii. Author's library.

At an early date the Christian Church registered its
opposition to the practice of wearing amulets. At the
Council of Laodicea, held in 355 A.D., it was decreed, in
the thirty-fourth canon, that priests and clerks must be
neither enchanters, mathematicians, nor astrologers, and
that they must not make "what are called amulets," for
these were fetters of the soul, and all who wore them

should be cast out of the church.[20] This emphatic condemnation of the prevailing usage was not so much a
protest against superstition *per se* as against pagan
superstition, for almost if not all the amulets in use in
the early centuries of our era bore heathen or heretical
symbols or inscriptions. In later times the invincible
tendency to wear objects of this character found expression in the use of those associated with Christian belief,
such, for instance, as relics of the saints, medallions
blessed by the priest, etc.

The amulets of the Jews differed in many respects
from those used by Christians. The Mosaic prohibition
of representations of human or animal forms imposed
great restrictions upon the employment of engraved
gems, and the Jew was only permitted to wear or carry
those bearing merely characters of mystic or symbolic
significance. In talmudic times amulets were sometimes
hidden in a hollow staff, and they were believed to have
more power when concealed from view in this way.
They were like concealed weapons, and it was said that,
as a father might give such an amulet to a son, so God
had given the Law to Israel for its protection.[21]

In the Old French didactic poem, the *Roman de la
Rose,* composed in the twelfth century, appear traces of
the belief in the magic properties of precious stones.
Chaucer translated this poem into English in the fourteenth century and we quote the following lines from
his version. They describe the costume of the symbolical
figure, Riches.

---

[20] Histoire critique des pratiques superstitieuses; par un prêtre de
l'Oratoire," Paris, 1702, p. 320.

[21] Blum, "Das altjüdische Zauberwesen," Strassburg, 1898, p. 91.

Richesse a girdle hadde upon
The bokel of it was of a stoon
Of Vertue greet, and mochel of might.

That stoon was greetly for to love,
And til a riche mannes bihove
Worth al the gold in Rome and Fryse.

The mordaunt [22] wrought in noble wyse,
Was of a stoon full precious,
That was so fyn and vertuous,
That hool a man it coude make
Of palasye and of tooth-ake.[23]

At the trial, in 1232, of Hubert de Burgh, chief jus-
ticiar, one of the charges brought against him was that
he had surreptitiously removed from the English treasury an exceedingly valuable stone, possessing the virtue
of rendering the wearer invincible in battle, and had
given it to Llewellyn, King of Wales, the enemy of his
own sovereign, Henry III of England (1207–1272).[24]
This must have taken place about 1228, when Henry was
engaged in a war with the Welsh.

That precious stones could, under certain circumstances, lose the powers inherent in them was firmly believed in medieval times. If handled or even gazed upon
by impure persons and sinners, some of the virtues of
the stones departed from them. Indeed, there were those
who held that precious stones, in common with all created
things, were corrupted by the sin of Adam. Therefore,
in order to restore their pristine virtue it might become

---

[22] A projection serving to fasten down the belt.

[23] Compleat Works of Geoffrey Chaucer, ed. Skeat, Oxford, 1849,
vol. i, p. 139.

[24] Matthæi Paris, " Historia major," London, 1684, p. 318.

necessary to sanctify and consecrate them, and a kind of ritual serving this purpose has been preserved in several old treatises. The subject is sufficiently curious to warrant here the repetition of one of these forms. The stones which required consecration were to be wrapped in a perfectly clean linen cloth and placed on the altar. Then three masses were to be said over them, and the priest who celebrated the third mass, clad in his sacred vestments, was to pronounce the following benediction:[25]

The Lord be with us. And with thy spirit. Let us pray. Almighty God and Father, who manifestedst thy virtue to Elias by certain senseless creatures, who orderedst Moses, Thy servant, that, among the sacerdotal vestments, he should adorn the Rational of Judgment with twelve precious stones, and showedst to John, the evangelist, the famous city of Jerusalem, essentially constituted by the same stones, and who hadst the power to raise up sons to Abraham from stones, we humbly beseech Thy majesty since Thou hast elected one of the stones to be a dwelling-place for the majesty of Thy heart, that Thou wilt deign to bless and sanctify these stones by the sanctification and incarnation of Thy name, so that they may be sanctified, blessed, and consecrated, and may receive from Thee the effect of the virtues Thou hast granted to them, according to their kinds, and which the experience of the learned has shown to have been given by Thee; so that whoever may wear them on him may feel the presence of Thy power and may be worthy to receive the gift of Thy grace and the protection of Thy power. Through Jesus Christ, Thy Son, in whom dwells all sanctification, benediction, and consecration; who lives with Thee and reigns as God for all eternity, Amen. Thanks be to God.

Konrad of Megenburg also gives this benediction in his "Buch der Natur."

Luther tells the following humorous tale of a Jew who was a vender of amulets:

---

[25] "Le Grand Lapidaire" of Jean de Mandeville, Vienna, 1862, pp. 126–128.

There is sorcery among the Jews and their sorcerers think: " If we succeed, it is well for us; if we fail, a Christian is the sufferer; what care we for that ? " . . . But Duke Albert of Saxony acted shrewdly. When a Jew offered him a button, inscribed with curious characters and signs, and asserted that this button gave protection from cuts, thrusts, and shots, the Duke answered: " I will test that upon thyself, O Jew." Hereupon he led the man to the gate, hung the button at his neck, drew his own sword, and thrust the fellow through the body. " The same fate would have happened to me," said the Duke, " as has happened to thee." [26]

Ruskin, with his keen poetic insight into the working of natural laws, saw in the formation of crystals the action of both ''force of heart'' and ''steadiness of purpose.'' He thus found himself, consciously or unconsciously, in agreement with the old fancies which attributed a species of personality to precious stones. Just as the Hindu regarded an imperfectly shaped crystal as a bringer of ill luck to the owner, so Ruskin sees in such a crystal the signs of an innate ''immorality,'' if we may use this expression. Of a crystal aggregation of this type he writes as follows: [27]

Opaque, rough-surfaced, jagged on the edge, distorted in the spine, it exhibits a quite human image of decrepitude and dishonour; but the worst of all signs of its decay and helplessness is, that half-way up, a parasite crystal, smaller, but just as sickly, has rooted itself in the side of the larger one, eating out a cavity round its root, and then growing backwards, or downwards, contrary to the direction of the main crystal. Yet I cannot trace the least difference in purity of substance between the first most noble stone, and this ignoble and dissolute one. The impurity of the last is in its will or want of will.

There is established a very pretty custom of assigning to the various masculine and feminine Christian

---

[26] Güdermann, " Das jüdische Unterrichtswesen," Wien, 1873, p. 225.

[27] " Ethics of the Dust," New York, 1886, p. 96.

names a particular gem, and such name-gems are often set together with natal and talismanic gems and with gems of one's patron saint. It is considered an exceedingly good omen when it happens that all three gems are of the same sort.

GEMS FOR FEMININE NAMES.

Adelaide	Andalusite
Agnes	Agate
Alice	Alexandrite
Anne	Amber
Beatrice	Basalt
Belle	Bloodstone
Bertha	Beryl
Caroline	Chalcedony
Catherine	Cat's-eye
Charlotte	Carbuncle
Clara	Carnelian
Constance	Crystal
Dorcas	Diamond
Dorothy	Diaspore
Edith	Eye-agate
Eleanor	Elæolite
Elizabeth	Emerald
Ellen	Essonite
Emily	Euclase
Emma	Epidote
Florence	Fluorite
Frances	Fire-opal
Gertrude	Garnet
Gladys	Golden Beryl
Grace	Grossularite
Hannah	Heliotrope
Helen	Hyacinth

Irene .... Iolite

Jane .... Jacinth
Jessie .... Jasper
Josephine .... Jadeite
Julia .... Jade

Louise .... Lapis-lazuli
Lucy........................ Lepidolite

Margaret .... Moss-agate
Martha .... Malachite
Marie .... Moldavite
Mary .... Moonstone

Olive .... Olivine

Pauline .... Pearl

Rose .... Ruby

Sarah .... Spodumene
Susan .... Sapphire

Therese .... Turquoise

GEMS FOR MASCULINE NAMES.

Abraham .... Aragonite
Adolphus .... Albite
Adrian .... Andalusite
Albert .... Agate
Alexander .... Alexandrite
Alfred .... Almandine
Ambrose .... Amber
Andrew .... Aventurine
Archibald .... Axinite
Arnold...................... Aquamarine
Arthur .....,.............. Amethyst
Augustus .... Agalmatolite

Benjamin .... Bloodstone
Bernard .... Beryl

Charles	Chalcedony
Christian	Crystal
Claude	Cyanite
Clement	Chrysolite
Conrad	Crocidolite
Constantine	Chrysoberyl
Cornelius	Cat's-eye
Dennis	Demantoid
Dorian	Diamond
Edmund	Emerald
Edward	Epidote
Ernest	Euclase
Eugene	Essonite
Ferdinand	Feldspar
Francis	Fire-opal
Frederick	Fluorite
George	Garnet
Gilbert	Gadolinite
Godfrey	Gagates
Gregory	Grossularite
Gustavus	Galactides
Guy	Gold quartz
Henry	Heliolite
Herbert	Hyacinth
Horace	Harlequin opal
Hubert	Heliotrope
Hugh	Heliodor
Humphrey	Hypersthene
James	Jade
Jasper	Jasper
Jerome	Jadeite
John	Jacinth
Joseph	Jargoon
Julius	Jet

4

Lambert .... Labradorite
Lawrence .... Lapis-lazuli
Leo......................... Lepidolite
Leonard .... Loadstone

Mark .... Malachite
Matthew .... Moonstone
Maurice .... Moss-agate
Michael .... Microcline

Nathan .... Natrolite
Nicholas .... Nephrite

Oliver .... Onyx
Osborne .... Orthoclase
Osmond .... Opal
Oswald .... Obsidian

Patrick .... Pyrope
Paul .... Pearl
Peter .... Porphyry
Philip .... Prase

Ralph .... Rubellite
Raymond .... Rose-quartz
Richard .... Rutile
Robert .... Rock-crystal
Roger...................... Rhodonite
Roland .... Ruby

Stephen .... Sapphire

Theodore .... Tourmaline
Thomas .... Topaz

Valentine .... Vesuvianite
Vincent .... Verd-antique

Walter .... Wood-opal
William.................... Willemite

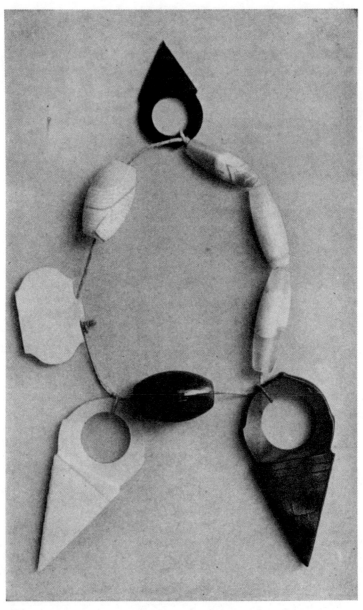

AFRICAN AGATE CHARMS.
Made of Brazilian agate at Oberstein, Germany, for African trade.   Field Museum, Chicago.

III

On the Talismanic Use of Special Stones[1]

Agate

THE author of "Lithica" celebrates the merits of the agate in the following lines:[2]

> Adorned with this, thou woman's heart shall gain,
> And by persuasion thy desire obtain;
> And if of men thou aught demand, shalt come
> With all thy wish fulfilled rejoicing home.

This idea is elaborated by Marbodus, Bishop of Rennes, in the eleventh century, who declares that agates make the wearers agreeable and persuasive and also give them the favor of God.[3] Still other virtues are recounted by Camillo Leonardo, who claims that these stones give victory and strength to their owners and avert tempests and lightning.[4]

The agate possessed some wonderful virtues, for its wearer was guarded from all dangers, was enabled to vanquish all terrestrial obstacles and was endowed with a bold heart; this latter prerogative was presumably the

---

[1] See also the writer's pamphlet: "The Folk-Lore of Precious Stones," Chicago, 1894; a paper read before the Folk-Lore Congress held at the World's Columbian Exhibition, and describing the Kunz Collection exhibited in the Anthropological Building there. This collection is now in the Field Museum, Chicago.

[2] King's version in his "Natural History of Precious Stones," London, 1865, p. 392.

[3] Marbodei, "De lapidibus," Friburgi, 1531, fol. 10.

[4] Camilli Leonardi, "Speculum lapidum," Venetia, 1502, fol. 22.

secret of his success. Some of these wonder-working
agates were black with white veins, while others again
were entirely white.[5]

The wearing of agate ornaments was even believed to
be a cure for insomnia and was thought to insure pleasant dreams. In spite of these supposed advantages, Cardano asserts that while wearing this stone he had many
misfortunes which he could not trace to any fault or
error of his own. He, therefore, abandoned its use;
although he states that it made the wearer more prudent
in his actions.[6] Indeed, Cardano appears to have tested
the talismanic worth of gems according to a plan of his
own,—namely, by wearing them in turn and noting the
degree of good or ill fortune he experienced. By this
method he apparently arrived at positive results based
on actual experience; but he quite failed to appreciate
the fact that no real connection of any kind existed between the stones and their supposed effects. In another
treatise this author takes a somewhat more favorable
view of the agate, and proclaims that all varieties render
those who wear them "temperate, continent, and cau-
tious; therefore they are all useful for acquiring riches.[7]

According to the text accompanying a curious print
published in Vienna in 1709, the attractive qualities of
the so-called coral-agate were to be utilized in an air-
ship, the invention of a Brazilian priest. Over the head
of the aviator, as he sat in the air-ship, there was a network of iron to which large coral-agates were attached.

---

[5] Albertus Magnus, " Le Grand Albert des secretz des vertus des
Herbes, Pierres et Bestes. Et aultre livre des Merveilles du Monde,
d'aulcuns effetz causez daulcunes bestes," Turin, Bernard du mont du
Chat (c. 1515). Liv. ii, fol. 8 recto.

[6] Cardani, " De subtilitate," Basileæ, 1560, p. 460.

[7] Cardani, " De gemmis," Basileæ, 1585, p. 323.

These were expected to help in drawing up the ship, when, through the heat of the sun's rays, the stones had acquired magnetic power. The main lifting force was

AN AIR-SHIP OF 1709.

In the network above the figure were to be set coral-agates, supposed to possess such magnetic powers as to keep the craft aloft. From Valentini, "Museum Museorum," Pt. III, Franckfurt am Mayn, 1714, p. 35. Author's library.

provided by powerful magnets enclosed in two metal spheres; how the magnets themselves were to be raised is not explained.[8]

---

[8] Valentini, "Museum museorum oder die vollständige Schau-Bühne," Franckfurt am Mayn, 1714, vol. ii, pt. 3, p. 34; figure of airship on p. 35.

About the middle of the past century, the demand for agate amulets was so great in the Soudan that the extensive agate-cutting establishments at Idar and Oberstein in Germany were almost exclusively busied with filling orders for this trade. Brown or black agates having a white ring in the centre were chiefly used for the fabrication of these amulets, the white ring being regarded as a symbol of the eye. Hence the amulets were supposed to neutralize the power of the Evil Eye, or else to be emblematic of the watchfulness of a guardian spirit. The demand for these amulets has fallen off greatly, but when it was at its height single firms exported them to the value of 40,000 thalers ($30,-000) annually, the total export amounting to hundreds of thousands of thalers. Even at present a considerable trade in these objects is still carried on. That there is a fashion in amulets is shown by the fact that, while red, white, and green amulets are in demand on the west coast of Africa, only white stones are favored for this use in Northern Africa.

Alexandrite

There are a few talismanic stones which have gained their repute in our time, notably the alexandrite, a variety of chrysoberyl found in Russia, in the emerald mines on the Takowaya, in the Ural region. The discovery of this variety is stated to have been made in 1831 on the day Alexander II (then heir-apparent) reached his majority, and it was therefore named alexandrite, by Nordenskjöld, the mineralogist. The stone as found in gem form rarely weighs over from one to three carats, and is characterized by a marked pleochroism of a splendid green changing to a beautiful columbine red. But in Ceylon much larger gems are found, some few weighing

1. Amber ornament, perforated, from Assyrian grave.
2. Amber ring ornament from Pompeii.
3. Large annular bead of amber from Mexico. Aztec work.
4. Amber wedding necklace. Eighteenth century. Baltic Provinces.
5. Amber beads. Worn by African natives.

60 carats each, although rarely of more than one or two carats. The color is of a darker and more bottle-like green, and the change by night renders them darker and more granitized than the Russian stones, which are extremely rare. As red and green are the Russian national colors, the alexandrite has become a great favorite with the Russians, and is looked upon as a stone of good omen in that country. Such, however, is its beauty as a gem that its fame is by no means confined to Russia, and it is eagerly sought in other lands as well.

Amber

Amber was one of the first substances used by man for decoration, and it was also employed at a very early period for amulets and for medicinal purposes. More or less shapeless pieces of rough amber, marked with circular depressions, have been found in Prussia, Schleswig-Holstein, and Denmark, in deposits of the Stone Age. These depressions are sometimes regularly disposed and at other times irregularly, and seem intended to imitate similar depressions found in large stones and rocks, often the work of man's hand, but occasionally the result of natural causes. In Hoernes' opinion they marked the resting place of the spirit or spirits believed to animate the stone, and hence it is probable that the amber fragments were used as talismans or amulets.[9]

For the ancient Greek poets, the grains of amber were the tears annually shed over the death of their brother Phaëthon by the Heliades after grief had meta-

---

[9] Hoernes, "Urgeschichte der bildenden Kunst," Vienna, 1898, p. 376. Figured in S. Muller's "Ordn. af Danm. Olds.," i, Pl. XV, Figs. 252 sq.

morphosed them into poplars growing on the banks of the Eridanus (the modern river Po).[10] In a lost tragedy of Sophocles, he saw the origin of amber in the tears shed over the death of Meleager by certain Indian birds. For Nicias it was the "juice" or essence of the brilliant rays of the setting sun, congealed in the sea and then cast up upon the shore. A more prosaic explanation likened amber to resin, and regarded it as being an exudation from the trunks of certain trees. Indeed, the poetic fancy we have just noted is the same idea clothed in a metaphorical or mythological form. Another fancy represented amber to be the solidified urine of the lynx, hence one of its names, *lyncurius*.[11]

THE TREE THAT EXUDES AMBER.
From the "Hortus Sanitatis," of Johannis de Cuba [Strassburg, Jean Pryss, ca. 1483]; De lapidibus, cap. lxx. Author's library.

The brilliant and beautiful yellow of certain ambers and the fact that this material was very easily worked served to make its use more general, and it soon became a favorite object of trade and barter between the peoples of the Baltic Coast and the more civilized peoples to the

---

[10] Ovidii, "Metamorphoses," lib. ii, 11. 340 sqq. Some have proposed to read Redanus instead of Eridanus and have seen in the former name the designation of a stream flowing into the Vistula.

[11] Plinii, "Naturalis Historia," lib. xxxvii, cap. 7.

south. Schliemann found considerable amber from the
Baltic in the graves of Mycenæ, and the frequent allusions to it in the works of Latin authors of the first and
succeeding centuries testify to its popularity in the
Roman world.

Probably the very earliest allusion in literature to
the ornamental use of amber appears in Homer's Odys-
sey,[12] where we read:

> Eurymachus
> Received a golden necklace, richly wrought,
> And set with amber beads, that glowed as if
> With sunshine. To Eurydamas there came
> A pair of ear-rings, each a triple gem,
> Daintily fashioned and of exquisite grace.
> Two servants bore them.

Amber ingeniously carved into animal forms has been
discovered in tumuli at Indersoen, Norway.[13] These
curious objects were worn as amulets, and the peculiar
forms were supposed to enhance the power of the material, giving it special virtues and rendering it of greater
value and efficacy.

Pieces of amber with singular natural markings were
greatly esteemed, especially when these markings suggested the initials of the name of some prominent person.
Thus, we are told that Friedrich Wilhelm I of Prussia
paid to a dealer a high price for a piece of amber on
which appeared his initials. The same dealer had another piece on which he read the initials of Charles XII
of Sweden. When he received the news of this king's
death, he bitterly lamented having lost the opportunity
of selling him amber for a high price. But he was
cleverly consoled by Nathaniel Sendal, the relator of the

---

[12] Bk. xviii, 11, 295–298, trans. of William Cullen Bryant.
[13] Du Chaillu, " The Viking Age," New York, 1889, vol. ii, p. 314.
(Figs. 1210, 1211, 1212.)

story, who easily persuaded the dealer that the markings could just as well signify the initials of some other name. Sendal adduces this as a proof that the letters read on such pieces of amber were as much the product of the observer's imagination as of the markings on the material.[14] Those who secured amber so mysteriously marked by Nature's hand probably felt that they had obtained a talisman of great power, especially destined for their use.

Amethyst

While the special and traditional virtue of the amethyst was the cure of drunkenness, many other qualities were attributed to this stone in the fifteenth century. For Leonardo,[15] it had the power to control evil thoughts, to quicken the intelligence, and to render men shrewd in business matters. An amethyst worn on the person had a sobering effect, not only upon those who had partaken too freely of the cup that intoxicates, but also upon those over-excited by the love-passion. Lastly, it preserved soldiers from harm and gave them victory over their enemies, and was of great assistance to hunters in the capture of wild animals. The amethyst shared with many other stones the power to preserve the wearer from contagion.[16]

A pretty legend in regard to the amethyst has been happily treated in French verse. The god Bacchus, offended at some neglect that he had suffered, was determined to avenge himself, and declared that the first person he should meet, when he and his train passed along, should be devoured by his tigers. Fate willed it that this

[14] Sendelii, " Electrologiæ," Elbingæ, 1725, Pt. I, p. 12, note.

[15] Camilli Leonardi, " Speculum lapidum," Venetia, 1502, fol. 22.

[16] Johannis de Cuba, " Hortus Sanitatis," [Strassburg, 1483] tractatus de lapibus, cap. vii.

luckless mortal was a beautiful and pure maiden named Amethyst, who was on her way to worship at the shrine of Diana. As the ferocious beasts sprang toward her, she sought the protection of the goddess, and was saved from a worse fate by being turned into a pure white stone. Recognizing the miracle and repenting of his cruelty, Bacchus poured the juice of the grape as a libation over the petrified body of the maiden, thus giving to the stone the beautiful violet hue that so charms the beholder's eye.[17]

From the various descriptions of this stone given by ancient writers, it appears that one of the varieties was probably the purple almandine or Indian garnet, and it is not improbable that we have here the reason for the name amethyst and for the supposed virtue of the stone in preserving from drunkenness. For if water were poured into a vessel made of a reddish stone, the liquid would appear like wine, and could nevertheless be drunk with impunity.

𝔅𝔢𝔯𝔶𝔩

Arnoldus Saxo, writing about 1220, after reciting the virtues of the beryl as given by Marbodus, after Evax and Isidorus, reports in addition that the stone gave help against foes in battle or in litigation; the wearer was rendered unconquerable and at the same time amiable, while his intellect was quickened and he was cured of laziness.[18] In the old German translation of Thomas de Cantimpré's "De Proprietatibus Rerum," we read that

---

[17] Belleau, "Œuvres poétiques," ed. Marty-Laveaux, Paris, 1878, vol. ii, pp. 172 sqq. The poem in which this tale occurs is the "Amours et nouveaux eschanges des pierres précieuses," written in 1576 and dedicated to Henri III.

[18] Rose, "Aristotles de lapidibus und Arnoldus Saxo," in Zeitschr. für D. Alt., New Series, vol. vi, p. 431.

the beryl reawakens the love of married people (er hat auch die art daz er der elaut lieb wiederpringt).[19]

Bloodstone

The heliotrope or bloodstone was supposed to impart a reddish hue to the water in which it was placed, so that when the rays of the sun fell upon the water they gave forth red reflections. From this fancy was developed the strange exaggeration that this stone had the power to turn the sun itself a blood-red, and to cause t h u n d e r, lightning, rain, and tempest. The old treatise of Damigeron relates this of the bloodstone, adding t h a t it announced future events by producing rain and by "a u d i b l e oracles." Probably t h e conjurors, before proceeding to use the stone for their incan-

Capitulum.rc.

A PRACTICAL TEST OF THE VIRTUES OF THE BLOODSTONE TO PREVENT NOSE-BLEED.

From the "Hortus Sanitatis" of Johannis de Cuba [Strassburg, Jean Pryss, ca. 1483]; De lapidibus, cap. xc. Author's library.

tations, watched the heavens and waited until they noticed the signs of an approaching storm. They then interpreted

---

[19] Konrad von Megenberg, "Buch der Natur," ed. by Dr. Franz Pfeiffer, Stuttgart, 1861, p. 436.

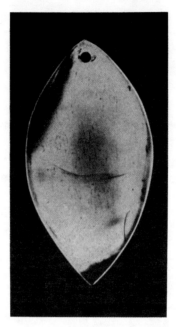

CHALCEDONY VOTIVE CHARM FROM MEXICO.
Aztec. Field Museum, Chicago.

CURIOUS ALTAR OF POWALAWA INDIANS OF ARIZONA.
The ceremonial objects are grouped around a crystal of rock-crystal in the centre. (See page 254.

the sounds of the wind and thunder in various ways, so as to give apt answers to the questions addressed to them touching future events. It is well known that the sighing of the wind, and, indeed, all those natural sounds which constitute the grand symphony of Nature, were interpreted by prophets and seers into articulate speech. Damigeron also declares that the bloodstone preserved the faculties and bodily health of the wearer, brought him consideration and respect, and guarded him from deception.[20]

In the Leyden papyrus the bloodstone is praised as an amulet in the following extravagant terms:

The world has no greater thing; if any one have this with him he will be given whatever he asks for; it also assuages the wrath of kings and despots, and whatever the wearer says will be believed. Whoever bears this stone, which is a gem, and pronounces the name engraved upon it, will find all doors open, while bonds and stone walls will be rent asunder.[21]

Carbuncle

The carbuncle was recommended as a heart stimulant; indeed, so powerful was its action, that the wearers were rendered angry and passionate and were even warned to be on their guard against attacks of apoplexy.[22] The blood-red hue of the stone also suggested its use as a symbol of the divine sacrifice of Christ on the cross. However, not only in Christianity was this stone used to illustrate religious conceptions, for the Koran affirms that the Fourth Heaven is composed of car-

---

[20] Pitra, " Specilegium Solesmense," Parisiis, 1855, vol. iii, p. 325.

[21] Kropatschek, " De amuletorum apud antiquos usu," Gryphiæ, 1907, p. 16.

[22] Cardani, " Philosophi opera quædam lectu digna," Basileæ, 1585, p. 323. " De gemmis."

buncle. In mythical fancies too this stone played its part, for dragon's eyes were said to be carbuncles.

Rumphius [23] states that in 1687 he was told by a chirurgeon that the latter had seen in the possession of one of the rulers in the island of Amboin a carbuncle said to have been brought by a serpent. The story ran that this ruler, when a child, had been placed by his mother in a hammock attached to two branches of a tree. While there a serpent crept up to him and dropped a stone upon his body. In gratitude for this gift the parents of the child fed and cared for the serpent. The stone is described as having been of a warm yellow hue, verging on red; it shone so brightly at night that a room could be illuminated by it. It eventually passed into the possession of a King of Siam.

Carnelian

Talisman ist Karneol
Gläubigen bringt er Glück und Wohl;
Steht er gar auf Onyx' Grunde,
Küss' ihm mit geweihtem Munde!
Alles Übel treibt er fort,
Schützet dich und schützt den Ort;
Wenn das eingegrabene Wort
Allah's Namen rein verkündet;
Dich zu Lieb' und Tat entzündet;
Und besonders werden Frauen
Sich am Talisman erbauen! [24]

Carnelian is a talisman,
It brings good luck to child and man;
If resting on an onyx ground,
A sacred kiss imprint when found.

---

[23] Rumphius, "Amboinsche Rariteitkamer," Amsterdam, 1741, p. 308.
[24] Goethe Westösterlicher Divan I, Segenspfänder.

It drives away all evil things;
To thee and thine protection brings.
The name of Allah, king of kings,
If graven on this stone, indeed,
Will move to love and doughty deed.
From such a gem a woman gains
Sweet hope and comfort in her pains.

The wearing of carnelians is recommended by the Lapidario of Alfonso X [25] to those who have a weak voice or are timid in speech, for the warm-colored stone will give them the courage they lack, so that they will speak both boldly and well. This is in accord with the general belief in the stimulating and animating effects produced by red stones.

On a carnelian is engraved in Arabic characters a prayer to keep away evil and to deliver the wearer from all the tricks of the devil and from the envious. The inscription reads in translation:

In the name of God the Just, the very Just!
I implore you, O God King of the World,
God of the World, deliver us from the devil
Who tries to do harm and evil to us through
Bad people, and from the evil of the envious.

Throughout all the East people are afraid of the envious. They believe that if you envy a person for his health or his wealth or any good thing he may have, he will lose it in a short time, and it is the devil who incites the envy of some people against others. So it is supposed that by wearing this stone, bearing this prayer against the envious, their envy will cease to do you harm.

The popularity of the carnelian as a talismanic stone

[25] "Lapidario del Rey D. Alfonso X," codice original, Madrid, 1881, fol. 77, p. 49.

among Mohammedan peoples is said to be due to the fact
that the Prophet himself wore, on the little finger of his
right hand, a silver ring set with a carnelian engraved
for use as a seal.   One of the most famous of the imâms,
Jafar, lent the weight of his authority to the belief in the
virtue of the carnelian, for he declared that all the desires of any man who wore this stone would be gratified.
Hence in Persia the name of one of the twelve imâms,
comprising Ali and his successors, is frequently engraved
on this stone.[26]

CARNELIAN SEAL, WORN BY NAPOLEON I, NAPOLEON III,
AND THE PRINCE IMPERIAL.

This most interesting seal is described by the Rev. C. W. King, the writer on Antique
Gems.   It is carnelian, octagonal-shaped, and upon it is engraved the legend: "The slave
Abraham relying upon the Merciful (God)."   Napoleon III wore it on his watch-chain.
He said about it: "The First Consul picked it up with his own hands during the campaign
in Egypt and always carried it about him, as his nephew did later."   The Prince Imperial
received it with the following message: "As regards my son, I desire that he will keep, as a
talisman, the Seal which I used to wear attached to my watch."   He carried the seal upon
a string fastened about his neck in obedience to the injunction of his father.   At the time
of his lamentable death it must have been carried off in South Africa by the Zulus, when
they stripped his body, and it has never been recovered.

An Armenian writer of the seventeenth century reports that in India the *lâl* or balas-ruby, if powdered and
taken in a potion was believed to banish all dark forebod-
ings and to excite joyous emotions.   To the carnelian was
attributed a virtue somewhat analogous to that ascribed
to the turquoise, as anyone wearing a carnelian was proof

---

[26] Hendley, "Indian Jewellery," London, 1909, p. 158.

against injury from falling houses or walls; the writer emphasizes this by stating that "no man who wore a carnelian was ever found in a collapsed house or beneath a fallen wall." [27]

Chalcedony

An ingenious though far-fetched explanation of the power attributed to chalcedony of driving away phantoms and visions of the night is supplied by Gonelli, writing in 1702. For him the source of this asserted power was to be found in what has been erroneously termed the alkaline quality of the stone. This dissipated the evil humors of the eye, thus removing the diseased condition of that organ which caused the apparitions to be seen.[28] However absurd this explanation may be, it nevertheless shows that the author put little faith in visible ghosts, and rightly enough recognized the purely subjective character of such phenomena.

Chrysoberyl

The cat's-eye variety of chrysoberyl, or precious cat's-eye, is used by the natives of Ceylon as a charm against evil spirits. As a proof of the high value set upon the gem in India, De Boot states that a cat's-eye estimated as worth ninety gold pieces in Lusitania was sold for six hundred in India.[29] Some of the finest specimens come from Ceylon.

---

[27] Arakel, " Livre d'histoire," chap. liii; transl. in Brosset, " Collection d'historiens arméniens," St. Pétersburg, 1874, vol. i, pp. 544, 545.

[28] Josephi Gonelli," Thesaurus philosophicus, seu de gemmis," Neapoli, 1702, p. 112.

[29] " Gemmarum et lapidum historia," Lug. Bat., 1636, p. 230.

5

Chrysolite

The "Serpent Isle," in the Red Sea, was stated by Agatharcides to be the source whence came the topaz (chrysolite); here, by the mandate of the Egyptian kings, the inhabitants collected specimens of this stone and delivered them to the gem-cutters for polishing.[30] These simple details are elaborated by Diodorus Siculus into the legend that the island was guarded by jealous watchers who had orders to put to death any unauthorized persons who approached it. Even those who had the right to seek the gem could not see the chrysolite in daytime; only after nightfall was it revealed by its radiance; the seekers then marked well the spot and were able to find the stone on the following day.[31]

From this Egyptian source, and possibly from others exploited by the Egyptians, have come the finest chrysolites (peridots, or olivines), the most magnificent examples of this gem. These found their way into the cathedral treasures of Europe, evidently by loot or trade at the period of the Crusades, and are generally called emeralds. Those most notable are in the Treasury of the Three Magi, in the great "Dom," or Cathedral at Cologne. Some of these gems are nearly two inches long.

In our own land beautiful specimens can be seen in the Morgan collection at the American Museum of Natural History and in the Higinbotham Hall in the Field Museum of Natural History, Chicago, Illinois.

Pliny quotes from Juba the tradition that the topaz (chrysolite) derived its name from the Island of To-

---

[30] Agatharcides, "De Mare Erythræo," §2. The topaz of the ancients was unquestionably the gem commonly called chrysolite at present (olivine, peridot).

[31] Diodorus Siculus, lib. iii, cap. 38.

pazos, in the Red Sea, the first specimen having been brought thence by the procurator Philemon, to Berenice, mother of Ptolemy II, Philadelphus. This monarch is said to have had a statue of his wife Arsinoë made from the stone.[32] If there be any foundation for this latter statement, the precious gift sent by Philemon must have been a mass of fluor-spar, or some similar material. More than three hundred years after Pliny's time, Epiphanius, evidently repeating another version of this tradition, states that the "topaz" was set in the diadem of the "Theban queen."

Chrysolite (olivine, peridot), to exert its full power, required to be set in gold; worn in this way it dispelled the vague terrors of the night. If, however, it were to be used as a protection from the wiles of evil spirits, the stone had to be pierced and strung on the hair of an ass and then attached to the left arm.[33] The belief in the virtue of the chrysolite to dissolve enchantments and to put evil spirits to flight was probably due to the association of the stone with the sun, before whose life-giving rays darkness and all the powers of darkness were driven away.

Chrysoprase

Wonderful things are told of the virtue of the chrysoprase, for Volmar states that, if a thief sentenced to be hanged or beheaded should place this stone in his mouth, he would immediately escape from his executioners.[34] Although we are not informed in what way this fortunate result was attained, it seems likely that the

---

[32] Plinii, "Naturalis Historia, lib. xxxvii, cap. 32.

[33] Marbodei, "De lapidibus," Friburgi, 1531, fol. 16.

[34] Volmar, Steinbuch, ed. by Hans Lambel, Heilbronn, 1877, p. 22.

stone was believed to make the thief invisible, and thus possessed a virtue often attributed to the opal.

A strange story regarding a magic stone reputed to have been worn by Alexander the Great is related by Albertus Magnus. According to this recital, Alexander, in his battles, wore a "prase" in his girdle. On his return from his Indian campaign, wishing one day to bathe in the Euphrates, he laid aside his girdle, and a serpent bit off the stone and then dropped it into the river.[35] Even Albertus, who is far from critical, admits that the story seems like a fable, and it probably belongs to a comparatively late period. As the term "prase" is used very loosely by early writers, this "victory stone" may have been an emerald or possibly jade.

Coral

The appreciation of coral as an ornament, or for amulets, seems to presuppose a certain development of civilization, for savage tribes greatly prefer glass ornaments. Many attempts have been made to introduce coral beads instead of glass beads among such tribes, but with no success, as the cheaper, but brighter, glass always commands a higher price.[36]

To still tempests and traverse broad rivers in safety was the privilege of one who bore either red or white coral with him. That this also stanched the flow of blood from a wound, cured madness, and gave wisdom, was said to have been experimentally proved.[37]

---

[35] Alberti Magni, " Opera Omnia," ed. Borgnet, Parisiis, 1890, vol. v, p. 43. De mineralibus, lib. ii, tract. 2.

[36] Bauer, " Edelsteinkunde," Leipzig, 1909, p. 750.

[37] Albertus Magnus, " Le Grand Albert des secretz des vertus des Herbes, Pierres et Bestes. Et aultre livre des Merveilles du Monde, d'aulcuns effetz causez daulcunes bestes," Turin, Bernard du mont du Chat (c. 1515). Liv. ii, fol. 9 recto

KABYLE JEWELRY.
Of Mediterranean coral and pearls. Field Museum, Chicago.

Coral, which for twenty centuries or more was classed among the precious stones, to retain its power as an amulet, must not have been worked, and in Italy only such pieces are valued for this purpose as have been freshly gathered from the sea or have been cast up by the sea on the shore. To exercise all its power against spells, or enchantments, coral must be worn where its brilliant color makes it conspicuous; if, however, it should by accident be broken, the separate pieces have no virtue, and the magic power ceases, as though the spirit dwelling in the coral had fled from its abode. The peasant women are careful to guard the corals they wear for a special purpose from the eyes of their husbands, for the substance is believed to grow pale at certain seasons, regaining its pristine hue after a short interval of time. Indeed, the women believe that the coral shares their indisposition with them. All this serves to show that a kind of vital force is believed to animate the material, gaining or losing in vigor according to certain conditions, and finally disappearing when the form is broken. These beliefs are all clearly traceable to the animistic ideas of primitive man.[38]

Diamond

The diamond is to the pearl as the sun is to the moon, and we might well call one the "king-gem" and the other the "queen-gem." The diamond, like a knight of old,—brilliant and resistant, is the emblem of fearlessness and invincibility; the pearl, like a lady of old, —pure and fair to look upon, is the emblem of modesty and purity. Therefore it does not seem unfitting that

---

[38] Bellucci, "Il feticismo primitivo in Italia," Perugia, 1907, pp. 22–25.

the diamond should be presented as a token to the pearl, and that pearls should go with the diamond. The virtues ascribed to this stone are almost all directly traceable either to its unconquerable hardness or to its transparency and purity. It was therefore thought to bring victory to the wearer, by endowing him with superior strength, fortitude, and courage. Marbodus [39] tells us it was a magic stone of great power and served to drive away nocturnal spectres; for this purpose it should be set in gold and worn on the left arm. For St. Hildegard the sovereign virtue of the diamond was recognized by the devil, who was a great enemy of this stone because it resisted his power by day and by night.[40] Rueus [41] calls it "a gem of reconciliation," as it enhanced the love of a husband for his wife.

Cardano [42] takes a more pessimistic view of the qualities of the diamond. He says:

It is believed to make the wearer unhappy; its effects therefore are the same upon the mind as that of the sun upon the eye, for the latter rather dims than strengthens the sight. It indeed renders fearless, but there is nothing that contributes more to our safety than prudence and fear; therefore it is better to fear.

The diamond was often associated with the lightning and was sometimes believed to owe its origin to the thunderbolt, but we do not recall having seen elsewhere the statement made in an anonymous Italian manuscript of the fourteenth century. Here it is expressly

[39] "De lapidibus," Friburgi, 1531, f. 8.
[40] St. Hildegardæ, "Opera Omnia," in Pat. Lat. ed Migne, vol. cxcvii, col. 1254.
[41] "De gemmis," Tiguri, 1566, f. 52.
[42] "Philosophi opera quædam lectu digna," Basileæ, 1585, p. 322. "De gemmis."

asserted that the diamond is sometimes consumed or melted when it thunders.[43] Certainly, that the same force that was supposed to have formed the stone should be able to dissolve it, is not an illogical idea. That the diamond can be entirely consumed at a high temperature was a fact not known in Europe in the fourteenth century, and therefore the belief in the destructive effect of the electric current must have arisen from superstitious or poetic fancies, and not from any vague conception of the true nature of the diamond.

In the Talmud we read of a gem, supposed to have been the diamond, which was worn by the high priest.[44] This stone served to show the guilt or innocence of one accused of any crime; if the accused were guilty, the stone would grow dim, but if he were innocent, it would shine more brilliantly than ever. This quality is also alluded to by Sir John Mandeville, who wrote:

It happens often that the good diamond loses its virtue by sin and for incontinence of him who bears it.

The Hindus classed diamonds according to the four castes. The Brahmin diamond gave power, friends, riches and good luck; the Kshatriya diamond prevented the approach of old age; the Vaisya stone brought success, and the Sudra, all manner of good fortune. On the other hand, in the treatise on gems by Buddhabhatta [45] we read:

A diamond, a part of which is the color of blood or spotted with red, would quickly bring death to the wearer, even if he were the Master of Death.

---

[43] Anonymous writer in Ital. MS. of the fourteenth century in the author's library; fol. 41 p. verso.

[44] See page 278 for description of this diamond by St. Epiphanius.

[45] Finot, "Les lapidaires indiens," Paris, 1896, p. 9.

The Arabians and Persians, as well as the modern Egyptians, agree in attributing to the diamond a wonderful power to bring good fortune, and Rabbi Benoni, a mystic of the fourteenth century, treating of its magic virtues, asserts that it produces somnambulism, and, as a talisman, so powerfully attracts the planetary influences that it renders the wearer invincible; it was also said to provoke a state of spiritual ecstasy. An alchemist of the same century, Pierre de Boniface, asserted that the diamond made the wearer invisible.

A curious fancy, prevalent in regard to many stones, attributed sex to the diamond, and it is therefore not surprising that these stones were also supposed to possess reproductive powers. In this connection Sir John Mandeville wrote:

> They grow together, male and female, and are nourished by the dew of heaven; and they engender commonly, and bring forth small children that multiply and grow all the year. I have oftentimes tried the experiment that if a man keep them with a little of the rock, and water them with May dew often, they shall grow every year and the small will grow great.

The following lines from a translation of the celebrated Orphic poem, written in the second century, show the high esteem in which the adamas was held at that time:

> The Evil Eye shall have no power to harm
> Him that shall wear the diamond as a charm,
> No monarch shall attempt to thwart his will,
> And e'en the gods his wishes shall fulfil.

This probably refers either to colorless corundum, the so-called "white sapphire," or to quartz. The writer is disinclined to believe that the ancients knew the diamond.

The ancient Hindu gem-treatise of Buddhabhatta asserts that the diamond of the Brahmin should have the whiteness of a shell or of rock-crystal; that of the Kshatriya, the brown color of the eye of a hare; that of the Vaisya, the lovely shade of a petal of the *kadali* flower; that of the Sudra, the sheen of a polished blade. To kings alone the sages assigned two classes of colored diamonds,—namely, those red as coral and those yellow as saffron. These were exclusively royal gems, but diamonds of all other shades could be set in royal jewels.[46]

A typical diamond is thus described in a Hindu gem-treatise: [47]

A six-pointed diamond, pure, without stain, with pronounced and sharp edges, of a beautiful shade, light, with well-formed facets, without defects, illuminating space with its fire and with the reflection of the rainbow, a diamond of this kind is not easy to find in the earth.

According to a wide-spread superstition, the talismanic power of a diamond was lost if the stone were acquired by purchase; only when received as a gift could its virtues be depended on.[48] The same belief is noted regarding the turquoise. The spirit dwelling in the stone was thought to take offence at the idea of being bought and sold, and was supposed to depart from the stone, leaving it nothing more than a bit of senseless matter. If, however, the diamond (or turquoise) were offered as a pledge of love or friendship, the spirit was quite willing to transfer its good offices from one owner to another.

The Talmud shows us that the Jewish Rabbis some-

---

[46] Finot, " Les lapidaires indiens," Paris, 1896, p. 8.

[47] Finot, l. c., p. 9.

[48] Konrad von Megenberg, " Buch der Natur," ed. by Dr. Franz Pfeiffer, Stuttgart, 1861, p. 433.

times endeavored to enliven their exhaustive discussions of ritual and legal questions by telling "good stories" to each other. One of these may be given as illustrating at once the wild improbability of some of these recitals and the belief in the wonderful magic virtues of the diamond: [49]

> R. Jehudah of Mesopatamia used to tell: Once while on board of a ship, I saw a diamond that was encircled by a snake, and a diver went to catch it. The snake then opened its mouth, threatening to swallow the ship. Then a raven came, bit off its head, and all water around turned into blood. Then another snake came, took the diamond, put it in the carcass, and it became alive; and again it opened its mouth, in order to swallow the ship. Another bird then came, bit off its head, took the diamond and threw it on the ship. We had with us salted birds, and we wanted to try whether the diamond would bring them to life, so we placed the gem on them, and they became animated and flew away with the gem.

It is said that the first large diamonds discovered by Europeans in South Africa were found in the leather bag of a sorcerer. Although large stones or fragments of rock are usually the objects of adoration as fetiches in Africa, any small stone that is wrapped in colored rags and worn on the neck may be regarded in the same way.[50] Several competent authorities state that these diamonds were the playthings of some Boer children.

Al Kazwini relates as follows the marvellous tale of the Valley of Diamonds: [51]

---

[49] New edition of the Babylonian Talmud, ed. and trans. by Michael L. Rodkinson, vol. v (xiii), Baba Batra, New York, 1902, p. 207.

[50] Ratzel, " Völkerkunde," Leipzig, 1885, vol. i, p. 36.

[51] Dr. Julius Ruska, " Das Steinbuch aus der Kosmographie des al-Kazwini," Beilage zum Jahresbericht 1894–5 der Oberrealschule Heidelberg, p. 35. See Aristoteles De Lapidibus und Arnoldus Saxo, ed. Rose, Z.f.D.A. New Series VI, pp. 364, 365, 389, 390. The " other writer " is probably Ahmed Teifashi.

" Aristotle [52] says that no one except Alexander ever reached the place where the diamond is produced. This is a valley, connected with the land Hind. The glance cannot penetrate to its greatest depths and serpents are found there, the like of which no man hath seen, and upon which no man can gaze without dying. However, this power endures only as long as the serpents live, for when they die the power leaves them. In this place summer reigns for six months and winter for the same length of time. Now, Alexander ordered that an iron mirror should be brought and placed at the spot where the serpents dwelt. When the serpents approached, their glance fell upon their own image in the mirror, and this caused their death. Hereupon, Alexander wished to bring out the diamonds from the valley, but no one was willing to undertake the descent. Alexander therefore sought counsel of the wise men, and they told him to throw down a piece of flesh into the valley. This he did, the diamonds became attached to the flesh, and the birds of the air seized the flesh and bore it up out of the valley. Then Alexander ordered his people to pursue the birds and to pick up what fell from the flesh."

" Another writer states that the mines are in the mountains of Serendib (Ceylon) in a very deep gorge, in which are deadly serpents. When people wish to take out the diamonds they throw down pieces of flesh, which are seized by vultures and brought up to the brink of the gorge. There such of the diamonds as cling to the flesh are secured; these are of the size of a lentil or a pea. The largest pieces found attain the size of a half-bean."

In his version of the tale, one form of which appears in the seventh voyage of Sindbad the Sailor, Teifashi states that the finest corundum gems were washed down the streams that flowed from Adam's Peak, on the island of Ceylon; in time of drought, however, this source of supply ceased. Now it happened that many eagles built their nests on the top of this mountain, and the gem-seekers used to place large pieces of flesh at the foot of the mountain. The eagles pounced upon these and bore them away to their nests, but were obliged to alight from

---

[52] The work on precious stones attributed to Aristotle was composed in Arabic probably in the ninth century.

time to time in order to rest, and while the pieces of flesh lay on the rock, some of the corundums became lightly attached to this, so that when the eagles resumed their flight the stones dropped off and rolled down the mountain side.[53]

These oft-repeated tales are explained by Dr. Valentine Ball as originating in the Hindu custom of sacrificing cattle when new mines were opened, and leaving on the spot a certain part of the meat as an offering to the guardian deities. As these pieces of meat were soon carried away by birds of prey, the legend arose that the diamonds were obtained in this way. This custom still prevailed in some parts of India when Dr. Ball wrote.[54]

The effect exercised by Hindu superstition on even the most enlightened Europeans of our day may be recognized in the fact that the gifted prima donna, Mme. Maeterlinck, the wife of the foremost living European poet, has confessed that she wears a diamond suspended on her forehead because her husband believes that this brings good fortune to the wearer. This forehead-jewel is characteristically Hindu and enjoys in India the reputation of being especially auspicious.

Emerald

The emerald was believed to foreshow future events,[55] but we do not learn whether visions were actually seen in the stone, as they were in spheres of rock-crystal or beryl, or whether the emerald endowed the wearer with a supernatural fore-knowledge of what was to come. As

---

[53] Teifashi, " Fior di pensieri sulle pietre preziose," Firenzi, 1818, p. 13.

[54] Proc. of the Royal Irish Academy, 2d Ser., Polite Literature and Antiquities, vol. ii, Dublin, 1879–1888, p. 303.

[55] Epiphanii, " De XII gemmis," Tiguri, 1565, fol. 5.

a revealer of truth, this stone was an enemy of all enchantments and conjurations; hence it was greatly favored by magicians, who found all their arts of no

SPECIMEN PAGE OF ITALIAN MANUSCRIPT OF THE FOURTEENTH CENTURY.

Containing an Italian version of the "De Mineralibus" of Albertus Magnus. On this page is the account of the emerald, set in a ring worn by King Bela IV of Hungary (1235–1270), that was fractured when he caressed his wife. Author's library.

avail if an emerald were in their vicinity when they began to weave their spells.[56]

---

[56] Morales, "De las piedras preciosas," Valladolid, 1604, fol. 101.

To this supernatural power inherent in the stone, enabling it to quicken the prophetic faculty, may be added many other virtues. If any one wished to strengthen his memory or to become an eloquent speaker, he was sure to attain his end by securing possession of a fine emerald.[57] And not only the ambitious, but also those whose hearts had been smitten by the shafts from Cupid's bow found in this stone an invaluable auxiliary, for it revealed the truth or falsity of lover's oaths. Strange to say, however, the emerald, although commonly assigned to Venus, was often regarded as an enemy of sexual passion. So sensitive was the stone believed to be in this respect that Albertus Magnus relates of King Bela of Hungary, who possessed an exceptionally valuable emerald set in a ring, that, when he embraced his wife while wearing this ring on his finger, the stone broke into three parts.[58]

In Rabbinical legend it is related that four precious stones were given by God to King Solomon; one of these was the emerald. The possession of the four stones is said to have endowed the wise king with power over all creation.[59] As these four stones probably typified the four cardinal points, and were very likely of red, blue, yellow, and green color respectively, we might conjecture that the other three stones were the carbuncle, the lapis-lazuli, and the topaz.

After stating that the emerald sharpens the wits and quickens the intelligence, Cardano declares that it therefore made people more honest, for "dishonesty is

---

[57] Marbodei, " De lapidibus, Friburgi, 1531, fol. 48; Camilli Leonardi, " Speculum lapidum," Venetia, 1502, fol. xliii.

[58] Fol. 55 recto of Ital. MS., 14th Century. Reference is to Bela IV (1235–1270). Lo reo dilugaria bela loqale in di nostri tempi regna.

[59] Weil, " Biblische Legenden," p. 225.

nothing but ignorance, stupidity, and ill-nature.'' The same writer adds that the stone was believed to make men economical and hence to make them rich, but of this he was very sceptical, since the experience of others as well as his own showed that the emerald possessed very little power in this direction.[60]

A talismanic emerald, once the property of the Mogul emperors of Delhi, has recently been shown in Europe. The stone is of a rich deep green, and weighs 78 carats. Around the edge in Persian characters runs the inscription: "He who possesses this charm shall enjoy the special protection of God."

Emerald sharpened the wits, conferred riches and the power to predict future events. To evolve this latter virtue it must be put under the tongue. It also strengthened the memory. The light-colored stones were esteemed the best and legend told that they were brought from the "nests of griffons." [61]

Gypsum

Gypsum when fibrous—the fibres being long and straight—is known as "satin spar." This material is frequently cut rounded, or *en cabochon,* across the fibres; sometimes it is cut in the form of beads, or of pear-shaped drops, which are mounted in earrings, scarf-pins, or necklaces. The material is frequently found in Russia, England, and elsewhere, and is cut in England or Russia. Some of the cut stones are mounted in brass, or gilded

---

[60] Cardani, " Philosophi opera quædam," Basileæ, 1585, p. 328. " De gemmis."

[61] Albertus Magnus, " Le Grand Albert des secrets des vertus des Herbes, Pierres et Bestes. Et aultre livre des Merveilles du Monde, d'aulcuns effetz causez daulcunes bestes," Turin, Bernard du mont du Chat (c. 1515). Liv. ii, fol. 11.

brass, and sold as luck stones at Niagara, the claim being made that the " satin spar " was taken from beneath the Falls at great peril, as occasionally small deposits of this kind of gypsum are found under the Falls.

From time to time small consignments of this material have been sent to Japan, as the Japanese value it possibly on account of its purity, or owing to the fact that it has the effect of the cat's-eye. It is quite cheap, and at the same time very soft, so that it can be scratched with the finger-nail. That found in Russia is of a golden-yellow or salmon color, and is worked into various ornaments, the one popular form being egg-shaped, and, because of their form, such objects are frequently given as Easter gifts. The same material is also known in Egypt, and is cut in the same egg form, the ornaments being called " Pharaoh's eggs," although just which Pharaoh this refers to is not stated. They are also believed to possess qualities of protection and to bring good fortune.

Hematite

The virtues of the hematite were praised in an ancient gem-treatise written by Azchalias of Babylon for Mithridates the Great, King of Pontus (d. 63 B.C.), a sovereign who was passionately fond of precious stones, and possessed a splendid collection of them, both engraved and unengraved. Azchalias, as cited by Pliny [62] taught that human destinies were influenced by the virtues inherent in precious stones, and asserted that the hematite, when used as a talisman, procured for the wearer a favorable hearing of petitions addressed to kings and a fortunate issue of lawsuits and judgments. It is a red oxide of iron, which when abraded shows a red streak; whence the

---

[62] " Naturalis historia," lib. xxxvii, cap. 60.

name hematite, from the Greek *haima*, "blood." As an iron ore and hence associated with Mars, the god of war, this substance was also considered to be an invaluable help to the warrior on the field of battle if he rubbed his body with it. Probably, like the loadstone, it was believed to confer invulnerability.

The high degree of skill possessed by the Pueblo workers is strikingly shown in a finely inlaid hematite cylinder found in Pueblo Bonito. The inlays are of turquoise and are designed to make the cylinder a conventional representation of a bird. The wings are indicated by turquoise inlays of pyramidal outline, curved so as to follow the curvature of the cylinder, the head being figured by a conical piece of turquoise attached to one end. This conical termination bore a small bird-figure carved in relief.[63] When we consider the difficulties the Indian workers had to overcome in the execution of this artistic task with the tools at their command, we can well realize that this object, probably an amulet, must have been considered very valuable, and was most likely the property of some one of high rank in the tribe or community.

Jacinth

The jacinth was more especially recommended as an amulet for travellers, because of its reputed value as a protection against the plague and against wounds and injuries, the two classes of perils most feared by those who undertook long journeys. Moreover, this stone assured the wearer a cordial reception at any hostelry he

---

[63] George H. Pepper, "The Exploration of a Burial-room in Pueblo Bonito, New Mexico," Putnam Anniversary Volume. New York, 1909, p. 239; Fig. 5.

visited.[64] It was said to lose its brilliancy and grow pale and dull if the wearer or any one in his immediate neighborhood became ill of the plague. In addition to these qualities the jacinth augmented the riches of the owner, and endowed him with prudence in the conduct of his affairs.[65]

St. Hildegard, the Abbess of Bingen (d. 1179), gives the following details as to the proper use of the *jachant* (jacinth) : [66]

> If any one is bewitched by phantoms or by magical spells, so that he has lost his wits, take a hot loaf of pure wheaten bread and cut the upper crust in the form of a cross,—not, however, cutting it quite through,—and then pass the stone along the cutting, reciting these words: " May God, who cast away all precious stones from the devil . . . cast away from thee, N., all phantoms and all magic spells, and free thee from the pain of this madness."

The patient is then to eat of the bread; if, however, his stomach should be too feeble, unleavened bread may be used. All other solid food given to the sick person should be treated in the same manner. We are also told that if any one has a pain in his heart, the pain will be relieved provided the sign of the cross be made over the heart while the above mentioned words are recited.

The wearer of a jacinth was believed to be proof against the lightning, and it was even asserted that wax that had been impressed by an image graven on this stone averted the lightning from one who bore the seal. That the stone really possessed this power was a matter of common report, it being confidently declared that in re-

---

[64] Marbodei, " De lapidibus," Friburgi, 1531, fol. 38.

[65] Cardani, " Philosophi opera quædam," Basileæ, 1585, p. 323. " De gemmis."

[66] S. Hildegardæ, Opera omnia; in Pat. Lat. ed. J. P. Migne, vol. cxcvii, Parisiis, 1855, col. 1251.

gions where many were struck by lightning, none who
wore a jacinth were ever harmed. By a like miracle it
preserved the wearer from all danger of pestilence even
though he lived in an air charged with the disease. A
third virtue was to induce sleep. Of this, Cardano states
that he was in the habit of wearing rather a large jacinth,
and had found that the stone "seemed to dispose somewhat to sleep, but not much." He adds, in explanation
of its slight efficacy, that his stone was not bright red,
nor of the best sort, but of a golden hue, differing much
from the best.[67]

𝔍𝔞𝔡𝔢

The name jade includes two distinct minerals, nephrite and jadeite. The former is a silicate of magnesia,
of exceedingly tough structure, and ranks 6.5 in the scale
of hardness, while jadeite, a silicate of alumina, is more
crystalline and not as tough as nephrite and has a hardness of 7. A variety having a rich emerald-green hue is
called by the Chinese *feits'ui,* "Kingfisher plumes"; it
is also denominated Imperial jade.

The original form of the Chinese character *pao,* signifying "precious,"consists of the outline of a house, within
which are the symbols of jade beads, shell, and an earthen
jar. This shows that at the very early time when these
characters were first used, the Chinese already collected
jade and employed it for personal adornment.[68] The
oldest form of the ideograph for "king" , 王, appears to
be the symbol for a string of jade beads, which are even

---

[67] Cardani, " De subtilitate," Basileæ, 1560, pp. 442–3.

[68] Chalfant, " Early Chinese Writing," Mem. of Carnegie Museum,
vol. iv, No. 1, Pittsburg, 1906, p. 10 and Pl. XX, No. 275. See also
Pl. X, No. 132; *pei,* " shell," " value," as shells were used as money
in very ancient times.

now used in China as insignia for high rank and authority.[69]

Jade amulets of many different forms are popular with the Chinese. One representing two men is called "Two Brothers of Heavenly Love," and is often given to friends. A phœnix of jade is a favorite ornament for young girls and is bestowed upon them when they come of age. To a newly-wedded pair is given the figure of a man riding on a unicorn and holding castanets in his hand; this signifies that an heir will be born in due time.

Such is the fondness of the Chinese for jade that those who can afford the luxury of its possession are wont to carry with them small pieces, so that they may have them always at hand; for they believe that, when handled, something of the secret virtue of the substance is absorbed into the body. When struck, jade is thought to emit a peculiarly melodious sound, which for the Chinese poet resembles the voice of the loved one; indeed, jade is termed the concentrated essence of love.

Fashioned into the form of a butterfly, a piece of jade acquires a special romantic significance in China, because of a Chinese legend which relates that a youth in his eager pursuit of a many-hued butterfly made his way into the garden of a rich mandarin. Instead of being punished for his trespass, the youth's unceremonious visit led to his marriage with the mandarin's daughter. Hence the figure of a butterfly is a symbol of successful love, and Chinese bridegrooms are wont to present jade butterflies to their fiancées.

A Chinese jade ornament constituting a child's amulet assumes a form approximating to that of a padlock. When this is attached to a child's neck, it is supposed to

[69] Chalfante, "Early Chinese Writing," Pl. XXII, No. 299.

bind the little one to life and protect it from all danger in infantile diseases.   A jade object of a different kind is sometimes used at nuptial feasts in China.   This is a cup having the form of a cock, and both bride and groom drink from it.   The form of this vessel is accounted for by a legend to the effect that when a beautiful white cock saw its young mistress, who had often petted it, throw herself into a well in a transport of despair at the loss of her lover, the faithful fowl sought and found death in the same way, so as not to be separated from its mistress.

Among the splendid Chinese jade carvings of the Woodward Collection is a curious symbolic ornament carved out of the rare *fei-ts'ui yü,* or "kingfisher-green jade," a rich emerald green jadeite with translucent green shading.   This ornament, executed in the beginning of the eighteenth century and believed to be a product of the Imperial Jade Works in Peking, figures the natural form of a so-called "hand-of-Buddha" citron, the finger-like protuberances of the fruit suggesting this strangely fanciful name.   The Chinese regard this as a most felicitous emblem, denoting at once a long life and abundance of riches for its enjoyment.   In the present carving the figure of a bat clinging to the foliage enveloping the fruit constitutes an added omen of good fortune, the Chinese character *fu* signifying at once "bat" and "happiness," another proof of what we are prone to call Chinese queerness, for with the superstitious of our race the bat is always looked upon as especially ill-omened.[70]

It is a well-known fact that many analogies have been found between the customs, usages, and products of the more civilized aborigines of the New World and those of

---

[70] " Catalogue of the Woodward Collection of Jades and other Hard Stones," by John Getz, Privately printed (New York), 1913, p. 11, No. 24.

the ancient Egyptians. Another instance is offered by the custom of placing a piece of *chalchihuitl* (jade?) or of some other green stone in the mouth of a noble, after his death, and calling this his heart. Among the lower classes a *texaxoctli,* a stone of small value, was used for the same purpose. We shall see that, in the Egyptian "Book of the Dead," directions are given for putting a semi-precious stone on or in a mummy, as a symbol, and designating this the heart of the deceased person. For the use of a green stone for this purpose by the ancient Mexicans, Mrs. Zelia Nuttall finds a reason in the two meanings of the Nahuatl word *xoxouhqui-yollotl,* which is used to signify a "free man," the literal meaning being a "fresh or green heart." Hence, the stone was a symbol of the rank of the deceased as well as of his heart.[71] The fact that jade celts have been found cut into several pieces is taken to indicate the high value placed upon this material; for it has been conjectured by Dr. Earle Flint, that a living chief would cut a piece from the jade he wore as a sign of his rank, in order to provide a suitable ornament or amulet for a dead kinsman.

To certain of the Chinese "tomb-jades"—that is, jade amulets deposited with the dead—has been given the name *han-yü,* or "mouth-jade," because these amulets, supposed to afford protection to the dead, were placed in their mouths. The Metropolitan Museum of Art in New York contains a fine collection of 279 specimens of jade from Chinese tombs, found within the past five or six years, and presented to the museum by Mr. Samuel F.

---

[71] Zelia Nuttall, " The Fundamental Principles of Old and New World Civilization," Cambridge, Mass., 1901, p. 195. Archæological and Ethnographical Papers of the Peabody Museum, Harvard University, vol. ii.

Peters. In color these jades are not especially attractive, for the material has acquired a brownish stain, due to the products of decomposition of the body, and also to the absorption of some of the chemical constituents of the other objects in the tomb, during the long period of time, in many cases a thousand years or more, since the bodies were consigned to their final resting place.

So multifarious are the uses to which jade is put by the Chinese, and so great is their admiration of its qualities, that they regard it as the musical gem *par excellence*. A series of oblong pieces of jade, of the same length and width, usually about 1.8 feet long and 1.35 feet wide, and numbering from 12 to 24, constitute a chime, the difference in the notes emitted by the material when sharply struck depending upon the varying thickness of the separate pieces. What is designated the "stone chime" used in court and religious ceremonials, is composed of 16 undecorated stones, while a series known as the singers' chime consists of from 12 to 24 pieces carved into fantastic shapes. This use of jade for the production of musical sounds dates far back in the Chinese annals. We are told that when Confucius was much troubled at the ill-success of his efforts to reform the Chinese morals of his day, he sought consolation in playing on the "musical stone." A peasant who noted this in passing by, exclaimed, as he heard the sounds: "Full indeed is the heart of him who beats the musical stone like that!" [72]

A jade ornament greatly favored by the Maoris of

---

[72] The Bishop Collection. "Investigations and Studies in Jade," New York, privately printed, 1906, vol. i, pt. iii, "Jade as a Mineral," by George Frederick Kunz, p. 117. Nos. 421 and 646 of the collection are excellent examples of this special jade.

New Zealand bore the name *hei-tiki* ("a carved image for the neck"). The ornaments of this class are very rude and grotesque representations of the human face or form, and were generally regarded as schematically figuring some departed ancestor. The head sometimes slanted right or left, so that the eyes, which were very large and occasionally inlaid with mother-of-pearl, were on an angle of forty-five degrees. These ornaments were prized not only as memorials, but because, having been worn by successive ancestors, they were supposed to communicate something of the very being of those ancestors to such descendants as were privileged to wear the treasured heirloom in their turn. In many cases, when the family was dying out, the last male member would leave directions that his *hei-tiki* should be buried with him, so that it might not fall into the hands of strangers.[73]

So rare was this New Zealand jade, known to the Maoris as *punamu* (green-stone), that the aid of a *tohunga,* or wizard, was regarded as necessary to learn where it could be found. On setting forth on a search for this material, the jade-seekers would take with them a *tohunga,* and when the party reached the region where jade was usually found the *tohunga* would retire to some solitary spot and would fall into a trance. On awaking he would claim that the spirit of some person, dead or living, had appeared to him and had directed to search in a particular place for the jade. He would then conduct

[73] The Bishop Collection. "Investigations and Studies in Jade," New York, 1906, vol. i, p. 12. Privately printed and edition limited to 100 copies. For a description of this monumental work see " The Printed Catalogue of the Heber R. Bishop Collection of Jade," by George Frederick Kunz, supplement to the Bulletin of the Metropolitan Museum of Art for May, 1906, Occasional Notes, No. 1..

the party to this place, where a larger or smaller piece of jade was invariably found. Of course the wizard had previously assured himself of the presence of the stone in the place indicated.

To this jade was given the name of the man whose spirit had revealed its location, and in many cases the grotesque form given to the stone was conceived to represent this man. We can easily understand the reverence accorded to the *hei-tikis* when we consider that they were not only prized as heirlooms, which had been handed down by the successive heads of the family, but were also believed to have been originally found in such a mysterious way.

When the head of the family died, his *hei-tiki* was generally buried with his body, but was exhumed after a shorter or longer time by the nearest male relative. As we have noted, if no representative of the family remained, the heirloom was allowed to remain in the grave. The fact that tribal or intertribal feuds sometimes arose in regard to the possession of a *hei-tiki* serves to prove the peculiar virtues ascribed to them.

While there can be little doubt that the heirloom was supposed to represent, in a very general way, the person whose name it bore, the particular form given it was largely determined by the natural shape of the mass, which was slowly and patiently fashioned into the form it eventually acquired. Though this was mainly due to the imperfect means of which the artist disposed, there was probably a conviction that the form of the natural stone was not the result of accident, but was in itself significant and required only to be rendered more clear and definite. The fabrication of the *hei-tikis* of the Maoris is said to have ceased in the early part of the last century. The greater number of those that have been collected in New Zealand appear to have been made from one hundred to one hundred and fifty years ago.[74]

Jasper

The jasper had great repute in ancient times as a rain-bringer, and the fourth century author of "Lithica" celebrates this quality in the following lines:[75]

> The gods propitious hearken to his prayers,
> Whoe'er the polished grass-green jasper wears;
> His parched glebe they'll satiate with rain,
> And send for showers to soak the thirsty plain.

Evidently the green hue of this translucent stone suggested its association with the verdure of the fields in an even closer degree than was the case with transparent green stones such as the emerald, etc. Another early authority, Damigeron, mentions this belief, and states that only when properly consecrated would the jasper do service in this way.[76] Jasper was also credited in the fourth century with the virtue of driving away evil spirits and protecting those who wore it from the bites of venomous creatures.[77] An anonymous German author of the eleventh or twelfth century recommends the use of this stone for the cure of snake bites, and states that if it be placed upon the bitten part the matter will come out

---

[74] See Fischer, " Ueber die Nephritindustrie der Maoris in Neusee-land," Archiv für Anthropologie, vol. xv, Braunschweig, 1884, pp. 463–466.

[75] King's version in his Natural History of Precious Stones, London, 1865, p. 382.

[76] Pitra, " Specilegium Solesmense," Parisiis, 1855, p. 328.

[77] Epiphanius, " De XII gemmis," Tiguri, 1565, fols. 7, 8.

from the wound.[78] Here the cure is operated, not by the absorbent quality of the stone, but by its supposed power to attract poison or venom to itself, thus removing the cause of disease.

A popular etymology of the Greek and Latin name for jasper is reported by Bartolomæus Anglicus, who writes that "in the head of an adder that hyght Aspis is founde a lytyl stone that is called Jaspis." The same authority pronounces this stone to be of "wunder vertue," and says that "it hath as many vertues as dyvers coloures and veines." [79] This is fully in accord with tradition, for, as color was at least as important as chemical composition in determining the talismanic or therapeutic worth of the different stones, the great variety of colors and markings in the different jaspers naturally indicated their use in many different ways.

𝕵et

Jet has been found among the palæolithic remains in the caves of the "Kesslerloch," near Thayngen, Canton Schaffhausen, Switzerland. The material was evidently derived from the deposits in Würtemberg and was shaped by flint chips. Quite possibly jet, as well as amber, was already regarded as possessing a certain talismanic virtue. Such ornaments, when worn, were believed to become a part of the very body and soul of the wearer, and were therefore to be guarded with jealous care.[80] In the

---

[78] Birlinger, "Kleinere deutsche Sprachdenkmäler," in Germania, vol. viii (1863), p. 302.

[79] Bartolomæi Anglici "De proprietatibus rerum," London, Wynkyn de Worde, 1495, lib. xvi, cap. 51, De Jaspide. Old English version by John of Trevisa.

[80] Hoernes, " Urgeschichte der bildenden Kunst," Wien, 1898, pp. 22, 24.

palæolithic cave-deposits of Belgium also, jet appears, the supply being in this instance derived from northern Lorraine. The fragments had been rounded and pierced through the centre.[81] This indicates their use as parts of a necklace or as pendants. Necklaces, bracelets, and rings were especially favored for the wearing of talismanic gems, since the stones could easily be so set that they would come in direct contact with the skin.

Jet was one of the materials used by the Pueblo Indians for their amulets. An exceptionally well-executed figure of a frog made of this material was found in Pueblo Bonito, in 1896, by Mr. Pepper. The representation is much more realistic than is the case in the other figures of this type from this region. Turquoise eyes have been inserted in the head of the figure and a band of turquoise surrounds the neck.[82]

Lapis-Lazuli

Both in Babylonia and in Egypt, lapis-lazuli was very highly valued, and this is shown by the use of its Assyrian name (*uknu*) in poetic metaphor. Thus, in a hymn to the moon-god Sin, he is addressed as the "strong bull, great of horns, perfect in form, with long flowing beard, bright as lapis-lazuli."[83] This may remind us of the "hyacinthine locks" of classical literature.

Lapis-lazuli, "a blue stone with little golden spots," was a cure for melancholy and for the "quartern fever,"

[81] Dupont, " L'homme pendant les âges de la pierre," Brussels, 1872, pp. 156 sqq.

[82] Pepper, " The Exploration of a Burial-room in Pueblo Bonito," Putnam Anniversary Volume, New York, 1909, p. 237.

[83] Ward, " Seal Cylinders of Western Asia," Washington, D. C., 1910, p. 121; citing Jastrow, " Religion," p. 303.

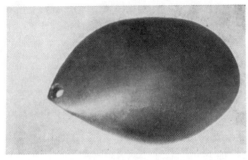

ARAGONITE PENDANT.
Used for votive purposes in Armenia.
Field Museum, Chicago.

PIECE OF NATURAL LOADSTONE.
Used in sixteenth century for medicinal purposes.

JASPER PENDANT.
Aztec Mexican. Used to stanch
blood.

an intermittent fever returning each third day, or each fourth day counting in the previous attack.[84]

Loadstone

We have the authority of Plato (Ion, 533 D) for the statement that the word *magnetis* was first applied to the loadstone by the tragic poet Euripides (480–405 B.C.), the more usual name being "the Heraclean stone." These designations refer to two places in Lydia, Magnesia and Herakleia, where the mineral was found.[85] Pliny states, on the authority of Nicander, that a certain Magnes, a shepherd, discovered the mineral on Mount Ida, while pasturing his flock, because the nails of his shoes clung to a piece of it.[86]

We are told by Pliny that Ptolemy Philadelphus (309–247 B.C.), planning to erect a temple in honor of his sister and wife Arsinoë, called in the aid of Chirocrates, an Alexandrian architect. The latter engaged to place therein an iron statue of Arsinoë which should appear to hang in mid-air without support. However, both the Egyptian king and his architect died before the design could be realized.[87] This story of an image held in suspense by means of powerful magnets set in the floor and roof, and sometimes also in the walls of a temple, is repeated in a variety of forms by early writers. Of

---

[84] Albertus Magnus, "Le Grand Albert des secretz des vertus des Herbes, Pierres et Bestes. Et aultre livre des Merveilles du Monde, d'aulcuns effetz causez daulcunes bestes," Turin, Bernard du mont du Chat (c. 1515). Liv. ii, fol. 11, recto.

[85] The Timæus of Plato, ed. by R. R. Archer-Hind, London, 1888, p. 302, note.

[86] Plinii, "Historia naturalis," Venetiis, 1507, fol. 269 verso, lib. xxxvi, cap. 16.

[87] Plinii, l. c., fol. 254, verso, lib. xxxiv, cap. 14.

course, there was no real foundation for such tales, as the thing is altogether impracticable.

The Roman poet Claudian (fifth century A.D.) relates that the priests of a certain temple, in order to offer a dramatic spectacle to the eyes of the worshippers, caused two statues to be executed,—one of Mars in iron, and another of Venus in loadstone. At a special festival these statues were placed near to each other, and the loadstone drew the iron to itself. Claudian vividly describes this:

> The priests prepare a marriage feast.
> Behold a marvel! Instant to her arms
> Her eager husband Cythereia charms;
> And ever mindful of her ancient fires,
> With amorous breath his martial breast inspires;
> Lifts the loved weight, close round his helmet twines
> Her loving arms, and close embraces joins,
> Drawn by the mystic influence from afar.
> Flies to the wedded gem the God of War.
> The Magnet weds the Steel: the sacred rites
> Nature attends, and th' heavenly pair unites.[88]

There was current as early as the fourth century a curious belief that a piece of loadstone, if placed beneath the pillow of a sleeping wife, would act as a touchstone of her virtue. This first appears in the Alexandrian poem "Lithica," and it has been thus quaintly Englished by a fourteenth century translator:

> Also magnes is in lyke wyse as adamas; yf it be sett under the heed of a chaste wyfe, it makyth her sodenly to beclyppe [embrace] her husbonde; & yf she be a spowse breker, she shall meve her oute of the bed sodenly by drede of fantasy.[89]

---

[88] King's metrical version in his "Natural History of Gems," London, 1865, p. 226.

[89] John of Travisa's version (made in 1396) of Bartholomæus Anglicus' "De proprietatibus rerum," London, Wynkyn de Worde, 1495, lib. xvi, cap. 43, De Magnete.

The same writer attempts an explanation of the popular fancy that when powdered loadstone was thrown upon coals in the four corners of a house, the inmates would feel as though the house were falling down; of this he says: "That seemynge is by mevynge [moving] that comyth by tornynge of the brayn."[90]

In classical writings the fascination exercised by a very beautiful woman is sometimes likened to the attractive power of the loadstone, as notably by Lucian,[91] who says that if such a woman looks at a man she draws him to her, and leads him whither she will, just as the loadstone draws the iron. To the same idea is probably due the fact that in several languages the name given to the loadstone indicates that its peculiar power was conceived to be a manifestation of the sympathy or love of one mineral substance for another. This is commonly believed to be the sense in which we should understand the French designation *aimant,* namely, as the participle of the verb *aimer,* "to love"; however, some etymologists prefer to derive the word from *adamas,* sometimes used in Low Latin for the loadstone, although properly signifying the diamond. It is certainly worthy of note that in two such dissimilar languages as Sanskrit and Chinese, the influence of this idea appears in the names given to the loadstone. In Sanskrit the word is *chumbaka* or "the kisser," and in Chinese *t' su shi,* or "the loving-stone." Chin T'sang Khi, a Chinese author of the eighth century, wrote that "the loadstone attracts iron just as does a tender mother when she calls her children to her.[92]

---

[90] Bartolomæi Anglici, " De proprietatibus rerum," l. c.

[91] Lucian, Imag. I.

[92] Klaproth, " Lettre à M. le Baron A. de Humboldt sur l'invention de la boussole," Paris, 1834, p. 20.

A rich growth of Mohammedan legends grew up about the exploits of Alexander the Great, a striking example being given on another page, and in one of them it is related that the Greek world-conqueror provided his soldiers with loadstones as a defence against the wiles of the jinns, or evil spirits; the loadstone, as well as magnetized iron, being regarded as a sure defence against enchantments and all the machinations of malignant spirits.[93]

In the East Indies it is said that a king should have a seat of loadstone at his coronation; probably because the magnetic influence of the stone was supposed to attract power, favor, and gifts to the sovereign. But it is not only in the Orient that magnetite is prized for its talismanic powers, for even in some parts of our own land this belief is still prevalent. Large quantities of loadstone are found at Magnet Cove, Arkansas, and it is estimated that from one to three tons are sold annually to the negroes to be used in the Voodoo ceremonies as conjuring stones. The material has been found in land used for farming purposes, and many pieces have been turned up in ploughing for corn; these vary from the size of a pea to masses weighing from ten to twenty pounds. They occur in a reddish-brown, sticky soil; their surface is smooth and brown and they have the appearance of water-worn pebbles. In July, 1887, an interesting case was tried in Macon, Georgia, where a negro woman sued a conjuror to recover five dollars which she had paid him for a piece of loadstone to serve as a charm to bring back her wandering husband. As the market value of this mineral was only seventy-five cents a pound, and the piece

---

[93] From El Kazwini's "Adjâïl el makluquat"; cited in marginal note, vol. i, pp. 310, 311, of El Damu's "Hayat el hayauân," Cairo, 1313 (1895).

was very small, weighing but a few ounces, the judge ordered that the money should be refunded.[94]

Malachite

For some reason not easy to fathom, malachite was considered to be a talisman peculiarly appropriate for children. If a piece of this stone were attached to an infant's cradle, all evil spirits were held aloof and the child slept soundly and peacefully.[95] In some parts of Germany, malachite shared with turquoise the repute of protecting the wearer from danger in falling, and it also gave warning of approaching disaster by breaking into several pieces.[96] This material was well known to the ancient Egyptians, malachite mines having been worked between Suez and Sinai as early as 4000 B.C.

The appropriate design to be engraved upon malachite was the image of the sun. Such a gem became a powerful talisman and protected the wearer from enchantments, from evil spirits, and from the attacks of venomous creatures.[97] The sun, as the source of all light, was generally regarded as the deadly enemy of necromancers, witches, and demons, who delighted in the darkness and feared nothing more than the bright light of day.

Moonstone

The moonstone is believed to bring good fortune and is regarded as a sacred stone in India. It is never displayed for sale there, except on a yellow cloth, as yellow

[94] Kunz, " Gems and Precious Stones of North America," New York, 1890, p. 192.

[95] Marbodei, " De lapidibus," Friburgi, 1531, fol. 51 ; Camilli Leonardi, " Speculum lapidum," Venetia, 1502, fol. xxxviii.

[96] Chiocci, " Museum Calceolarium," Veronæ, 1622, p. 227.

[97] De Boot, " Gemmarum et lapidum historia," Lug. Bat., 1636, p. 264, lib. ii, cap. 113.

7

is an especially sacred color. As a gift for lovers the
moonstone takes a high rank, for it is believed to arouse
the tender passion, and to give lovers the power to read
in the future the fortune, good or ill, that is in store for
them. To gain this knowledge, however, the stone must
be placed in the mouth while the moon is full.[98]

Antoine Mizauld [99] tells us of a selenite or moonstone
owned by a friend of his, a great traveller. This stone,
about the size of the gold piece known as the gold noble,
but somewhat thicker, indicated the waxing and waning
of the moon by a certain white point or mark which grew
larger or smaller as did the moon. Mizauld relates that
to convince himself of the truth of this he obtained possession of the stone for one lunar month, during which
time he sedulously observed it. The white mark first
appeared at the top. It was like a small millet-seed, increasing in size and moving down on the stone, always
assuming the form of the moon until, on reaching the
middle, it was round like the full moon; then the mark
gradually passed up again as the moon diminished. The
owner declared that he had "vowed and dedicated this
stone to the young king [Edward VI], who was then
highly esteemed because he had good judgment in regard
to rare and precious things."

Onyx

The onyx, if worn on the neck, was said to cool the
ardors of love, and Cardano relates that everywhere in
India the stone was worn for this purpose.[100] This belief
is closely related to the idea commonly associated with the
onyx,—namely, that it provoked discord and separated

---

[98] Marbodei, " De lapidibus," Friburgi, 1531, fol. 51.

[99] " Les secrets de la Lune," Paris, 1571.

[100] Cardani, " De subtilitate," lib. vii, Basileæ, 1560, p. 464.

lovers. The close union and yet the strange contrast between the layers of black and white may have suggested
this.

𝔓𝔶𝔯𝔦𝔱𝔢𝔰

Crystals of iron pyrites (pyrite, native iron disul-
phide) are sometimes used as amulets by the North

American Indians, and the
belief in their magic power
is attested by their presence
in the outfit of miscellane-
ous objects which the medicine-men use in the course
of their incantations. Because these gleaming yellow
crystals are occasionally
mistaken for gold, the
name "fool's gold" has
been popularly bestowed
upon them.[101]

Of this material the
a n c i e n t Mexicans made
wonderful mirrors, one side
being u s u a l l y polished
flat, while the other side
was strongly convex. Fre-
quently this side was curi-

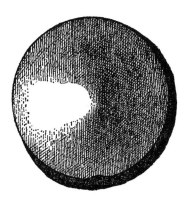

OBSIDIAN MIRROR, FROM OAXACA,
MEXICO. NOW IN TROCADÉRO
MUSEUM, PARIS.

See "Gems and Precious Stones of North
America," by George Frederick Kunz, New
York, 1890, p. 299.

ously carved with some symbolic representation as appears in the case of a pyrite mirror of the Pinard collection in the Trocadéro, Paris.[102]

---

[101] "Handbook of American Indians North of Mexico," ed. by
Frederick Webb Hodge; Smithsonian Inst.; Bur. Am. Ethn., Bull. 30;
Washington, 1910, Pt. 2, p. 331.

[102] Kunz, "Gems and Precious Stones of North America," New
York, 1890, pp. 299, 300.

Rock=crystal

The popular belief in his time as to the origin of rock-crystal is voiced by St. Jerome, when, using the words of Pliny, although not citing his authority, he says that it was formed by the congelation of water in dark caverns of the mountains, where the temperature was intensely cold, so that, ''While a stone to the touch, it seems like

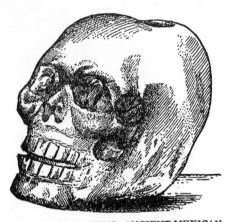

ROCK-CRYSTAL SKULL, ANCIENT MEXICAN
Weighing 475¼ oz. Troy. Now in the British Museum, London. From " Gems and Precious Stones of North America," by George Frederick Kunz, New York, 1890, p. 285.

water to the eye.'' This belief was evidently due to the fact that rock-crystal was so often found in mountain clefts and caverns. Symbolically, it signified that those within the portals of the Church should keep themselves free from stain and have a pure faith.[103]

The Chinese emperor Wu was devoted to the service of the gods and of the immortal spirits. He built many edifices for religious purposes, and all the doors of these

---

[103] Sancti Eusebii Hieronymi " Opera Omnia," ed. Migne, vol. iv, Parisiis, 1865, col. 545.

OBSIDIAN MASK, FROM THE FAYOUM, EGYPT.

Twelfth Dynasty. Late De Lesseps Collection. Collection of Mrs. Henry Draper. The obsidian is the typical stone of Mexico.

buildings were made of white rock-crystal, so that a flood of light poured into the interior. Although the Chinese texts call this material rock-crystal, it is possible that the name was applied to glass when that substance was but recently introduced into China.[104]

Regarding this same "rock-crystal" a humorous tale is related. Muan-fen, a mandarin who had a great terror of draughts, was once received in the palace by one of the Chinese emperors. The doors of the audience chamber were of rock-crystal and were tightly closed, but, because of the transparency of the material, they seemed to be wide open, and the emperor was greatly amused to note that Muan-fen was shivering with cold, although the temperature of the room was quite comfortable.[105]

An exceptionally fine specimen of Aztec work is a skull carved out of rock-crystal. It weighs 475¼ ounces Troy, and measures 8¼ inches in width.

Ruby

The ruby has many names in Sanskrit, some of them clearly showing that it was more valued as a gem by the Hindus than any other. For instance, it is called *ratnaraj*, "king of precious stones," and *ratnanâyaka*, "leader of precious stones;" another name, applied to a particular shade of ruby is *padmarâga*, "red as the lotus."[106]

The glowing hue of the ruby suggested the idea that an inextinguishable flame burned in this stone. From this fancy came the assertion that the inner fire could not

---

[104] Pfizmeier, "Beiträge zur Geschichte der Edelsteinen und des Goldes," Sitzungsbericht d. phil. hist. Kl., Wien, vol. lviii, 1868, p. 200.

[105] Pfizmeier, l. c., p. 201.

[106] Garbe, "Die indische Mineralien; Naharari's Rajanighantu, Varga XIII, Leipzig, 1882, p. 70.

be hidden, as it would shine through the clothing or through any material that might be wrapped around the stone.[107] If cast into the water the ruby communicated its heat to the liquid, causing it to boil. The dark and the star rubies were called "male" stones, the others, more especially, however, those of lighter hue, being considered as "female" stones. All varieties served to preserve the bodily and mental health of the wearer, for they removed evil thoughts, controlled amorous desires, dissipated pestilential vapors, and reconciled disputes.[108]

In the "Lapidaire" of Philippe de Valois, it is said that "the books tell us the beautiful clear and fine ruby is the lord of stones; it is the gem of gems, and surpasses all other precious stones in virtue." In the time of Marbodus (end of the eleventh century A.D.) the same proud place was assigned to the sapphire. The ruby is spoken of in similar terms in the "Lapidaire en Vers," where it is called "the most precious of the twelve stones God created when He created all creatures" By Christ's command the ruby was placed on Aaron's neck, "the ruby, called the lord of gems; the highly prized, the dearly loved ruby, so fair with its gay color."[109]

As with diamonds, rubies also were divided by the Hindus into four castes. The true Oriental ruby was a Brahmin; the rubicelle, a Kshatriya; the spinel, a Vaisya, and lastly, the balas-ruby, a Sudra. The possession of a *padmarâga*, or Brahmin ruby, conferred perfect safety upon the owner, and as long as he owned this precious stone he could dwell without fear in the midst of enemies

[107] Epiphanii, "De XII gemmis," Tiguri, 1565, fol. 5.
[108] Camilli Leonardi, " Speculum lapidum," Venetia, 1502, fol. xxvi.
[109] Pannier, " Les lapidaires français," Paris, 1882, pp. 246, 264, 295. Cited in Schofield, " The Pearl," Pub. of Mod. Lang. Asso. of Am., vol. xxiv, Pt. 4, p. 599.

and was shielded from adverse fortune. However, great care had to be taken to preserve this ruby of the first class from contact with inferior specimens, as its virtue would thereby be contaminated, and its power for good correspondingly diminished.[110]

The many talismanic virtues of the ruby are noted in the fourteenth century treatise attributed to Sir John Mandeville.[111] Here the fortunate owner of a brilliant ruby is assured that he will live in peace and concord with all men, that neither his land nor his rank will be taken from him, and that he will be preserved from all perils. The stone would also guard his house, his fruit-trees, and his vineyards from injury by tempests. All the good effects were most surely secured if the ruby, set in ring, bracelet, or brooch, were worn on the left side.

The gorgeous ruby, the favorite gem of Burma, where the finest specimens are found, is not only valued for its beauty, but is also believed to confer invulnerability. To attain this end, however, it is not thought to be sufficient to wear these stones in a ring or other piece of jewelry, but the stone must be inserted in the flesh, and thus become, so to speak, a part of its owner's body. Those who in this way bear about with them a ruby, confidently believe that they cannot be wounded by spear, sword, or gun.[112] As it is often remarked that the most daring and reckless soldiers pass unscathed through all the perils of war, we can understand that this superstition may sometimes appear to be verified.

---

[110] Surindro Mohun Tagore, "Mani Málá," Pt. I, Calcutta, 1879, p. 199.

[111] "Le grand lapidaire de Jean de Mandeville," from the ed. of 1561, ed. by J. S. del Sotto, Vienne, 1862, p. 8.

[112] Taw Sein Ko, communication from his "Burmese Necromancy."

Sapphire

The sapphire is noted as a regal gem by Damigeron, who asserts that kings wore it about their necks as a powerful defence from harm. The stone preserved the wearer from envy and attracted divine favor.[113] For royal use, sapphires were set in bracelets and necklaces, and the sacred character of the stone was attested by the tradition that the Law given to Moses on the Mount was engraved on tablets of sapphire.[114] While we should probably translate here "lapis-lazuli" instead of "sapphire," all such passages were later understood as referring to the true sapphire, which is not found in pieces of the requisite size.

In the twelfth century, the Bishop of Rennes lavishes encomiums upon this beautiful stone. It is quite natural that this writer should lay especial stress upon the use of the sapphire for the adornment of rings, for it was in his time that it was beginning to be regarded as the stone most appropriate for ecclesiastical rings. The sapphire was like the pure sky, and mighty Nature had endowed it with so great a power that it might be called sacred and the gem of gems. Fraud was banished from its presence and necromancers honored it more than any other stone, for it enabled them to hear and to understand the obscurest oracles.[115]

The traditional virtue of the sapphire as an antidote against poison is noted by Bartolomæus Anglicus, who claims to have seen a test of its power, somewhat similar to that recorded by Ahmed Teifashi of the emerald. In

---

[113] Pitra, "Specilegium Solesmense," Parisiis, 1855, vol. iii, p. 328.

[114] Epiphanii, "De XII gemmis," Tiguri, 1565, fol. 6.

[115] Marbodei, "De lapidibus," Friburgi, 1531, fols. 46, 47.

John of Trevisa's version this passage reads as follows: [116]

His vertue is contrary to venym, and quencheth it every deale. And yf you put an attercoppe [117] in a boxe and hold a very saphyre of Inde at the mouth of the boxe ony whyle, by vertue thereof the atter-coppe is overcome & dyeth as it were sodenly, as Dyasc. sayth [pseudo Dioscorides]. And this same I have assayed oft in many and dyvers places. His vertue kepeth and savyth the syght, & clearyth eyen of fylthe wythout ony greyf.

Voicing the general belief that the sapphire was en-dowed with power to influence spirits, Bartolomæus says that this stone was a great favorite with those who prac-tised necromancy, and he adds: "Also wytches love well this stone, for they wene that they may werke certen wondres by vertue of this stone." [118]

There was in the South Kensington Museum, in London, a splendid sapphire of a peculiar tint. In the daylight it shows a beautiful rich blue color, while by artificial light it has a violet hue and resembles an amethyst. In the eighteenth century this stone was in the collection of Count de Walicki, a Polish nobleman, and Mme. de Genlis used it as the theme of one of her stories, entitled "Le Saphire Merveilleux." Here the sapphire is used as a test of female virtue, the change of color indicating unfaithfulness on the part of the wearer. If the owner of the stone wished to prove that the subject of the test was innocent, she was made to wear the sapphire for three hours of daylight; but in the opposite case the test was so timed that it began in daylight and ended when the

---

[116] Bartolomæi Anglici, "De proprietatibus rerum," London, Wynkyn de Worde, 1495, lib. xvi, cap. 86, De Saphiro.

[117] Old English for spider.

[118] Bartolomæus Anglicus, l. c.

candles or lamps had been lighted. This sapphire, still known as the "Saphire Merveilleux," was for a time in the collection of the Duke of Orleans, who bore the name of Philippe Egalité during the French Revolution.

The star sapphire is that variety of sapphire in which, when the stone is cut and rounded off horizontal with the dome of the crystal, the light is condensed across the three lines of crystalline interference. Three cross lines produce a star which moves as a source of light, or as it is moved from the source of light. Star sapphires very rarely possess the deep blue color of the fine blue sapphire; generally the color is somewhat impure, or of a milky-blue, or else a blue-gray, or sometimes almost a pure white. The blue-gray, gray, and white stones frequently show a much more distinct star, possibly from the fact that there are more inclusions between the layers of the crystals than with the darker blue stones, as it is the set of interference bands that produces the peculiar light. Just as the eye agate was used in some countries to preserve against the Evil Eye, so the moving star is believed by the Cingalese to serve as a protection and a guard against witchcraft of all kinds.

The great Oriental traveller, Sir Richard Francis Burton, had a large star sapphire or asteria, as it was called. He referred to it as his talisman, for it always brought him good horses and prompt attention wherever he went; in fact, it was only in those places where he received proper attention that he would show it to the natives, a favor they greatly appreciated, because the sight of the stone was believed to bring good luck. The fame of Burton's asteria travelled ahead of him, and it served him well as a guiding-star. De Boot, writing in the seventeenth century, states that such a stone was called Siegstein (victory-stone) among the Germans.

The remarkable asteria, known as the "Star of India," in the Morgan-Tiffany Collection in the American Museum of Natural History, has a more or less indefinite historic record of some three centuries, but after its many wanderings it has now found a worthy resting-place in the great Museum. Its weight is 543 carats.[119]

The asteria, or star sapphire, might be called a "Stone of Destiny," as the three cross-bars which traverse it are believed to represent Faith, Hope, and Destiny. As the stone is moved, or the light changes, a living star appears. As a guiding gem, warding off ill omen and the Evil Eye, the star-sapphire is worn for the same reasons as were the *oculus mundi* and the *oculus Beli*. One of the most unique of talismanic stones, it is said to be so potent that it continues to exercise its good influence over the first wearer even when it has passed into other hands.

Sard

The sard was regarded as a protection against incantations and sorcery, and was believed to sharpen the wits of the wearer, rendering him fearless, victorious, and happy.[120] The red hue of this stone was supposed to neutralize the malign influence of the dark oynx, driving away the bad dreams caused by the latter and dispelling the melancholy thoughts it inspired.

---

[119] The subject of the origin, development and reform of the carat-weight has been fully treated by the author in the Trans. of the Soc. of Min. Engineers, 1913, pp. 1225–1245, " The New International Metric Diamond Carat of 200 milligrams."

[120] Marbodei, " De lapidibus," Friburgi, 1531, fol. 50, note of Pictor Villengensis.

Serpentine

The Italian peasants of to-day believe that pebbles
of green serpentine afford protection from the bites of
venomous creatures. These stones are usually green with
streaks or veins of white, and the name was derived from
their fancied resemblance to a serpent's skin. In addition to their prophylactic powers, if any one has been
bitten by such a creature, the stone, when applied to the
wound, is supposed to draw out the poison. Here, as
in the case of coral, the hand of man must not have shaped
the amulet; it should be in its natural state. As a general rule, however, the belief that the touch of any iron
instrument, such as the tool of the gem-cutter, destroys
the magic efficacy of the substance, is less firmly held in
regard to stones than in reference to coral.[121]

Topaz

See Chrysolite.

Turquoise

While there was a tendency to attribute the virtues
originally ascribed to one particular stone to others of
the same or similar color and appearance, certain stones
were regarded as possessing special virtues not commonly attributed to others. A notable instance of this is
the quality supposed to inhere in the turquoise. This
stone was known in Egypt from a very early period and
is later described by Pliny under the name of *callais*.
For Pliny, and for all those who derived their information from him or from the sources he used, the turquoise
only participated in the virtues assigned to all blue or

---

[121] Bellucci, " Il feticismo primitivo in Italia," Perugia, 1907, pp.
25, 26.

greenish-blue stones; but from the thirteenth century, when the name turquoise was first employed, we read that the stone possessed the power to protect the wearer from injury by falling, more especially from horseback; later, this was extended to cover falls from a building or over a precipice. A fourteenth century authority, the "Lapidaire" of Sir John Mandeville, states that the turquoise protected horses from the ill-effects resulting from drinking cold water when overheated by exertion, and it is said that the Turks often attached these stones to the bridles and frontlets of their horses as amulets. They are also so used in Samarcand and Persia. We might therefore be justified in supposing that the turquoise was originally used in the East as a "horse-amulet," and the belief in its power to protect from falls may have arisen from the idea that it rendered the horse more sure-footed and enduring. As the horse was often regarded as a symbol of the sun in its rapid course through the blue heavens, the celestial hue of the turquoise may have caused it to be associated in some way with the horse. We can only hazard this as a plausible conjecture.

Probably the earliest notice of the peculiar superstition in regard to the turquoise—namely, that it preserves the wearer from injury in case of falling—is contained in Volmar's thirteenth century "Steinbuch," where we read:

Whoever owns the true turquoise set in gold will not injure any of his limbs when he falls, whether he be riding or walking, so long as he has the stone with him.[122]

Anselmus de Boot, court physician of Emperor Rudolph II, tells a story of a turquoise that, after being thirty years in the possession of a Spaniard, was offered

---

[122] Volmar, "Steinbuch," ed. by Hans Lambel, Heilbronn, 1877, p. 19.

for sale with the rest of the owner's property. Every
one was amazed to find it had entirely lost its color;
nevertheless De Boot's father bought it for a trifling
sum. On his return home, however, ashamed to wear so
mean-looking a gem, he gave it to his son, saying, ''Son,
as the virtues of the turquoise are said to exist only when
the stone has been given, I will try its efficacy by bestow-
ing it upon thee.'' Little appreciating the gift, the recip-
ient had his arms engraved on it as though it had been
only a common agate and wore it as a signet. He had
scarcely worn it a month, however, before it resumed its
pristine beauty and daily seemed to increase in splendor.
Could we accept this statement as true we would have
here an altogether unique instance of the recovery by a
turquoise of the blue color it had lost.

Not long after, the powers of De Boot's turquoise
were put to the test. As he was returning to Bohemia
from Padua, where he had just taken his degree, he was
forced to traverse a narrow and dangerous road at night.
Suddenly his horse stumbled and threw him heavily to
the ground, but, strange to say, neither horse nor rider
was injured by the fall. Next morning, while washing his
hands, De Boot remarked that about a quarter of his turquoise had broken away. Nevertheless the stone did not
lose its virtue. Some time afterward, when the wearer
was lifting a very heavy pole, he felt all at once a sharp
pain in his side and heard his ribs crack, so that he
feared he had injured himself seriously. However, it
turned out that he had not broken any bones but had
simply strained himself; but, on looking at his turquoise,
he saw that it had again broken into two pieces.[123]

---

[123] De Boot, " Gemmarum et lapidum historia," Lug. Bat., 1636,
pp. 266–268.

A singular virtue ascribed to the turquoise was that of striking the hour correctly, if the stone were suspended from a thread held between the thumb and index-finger in such a way that a slight vibration would make the stone strike against the side of a glass. De Boot states that he made the experiment successfully, but he very sensibly explains the apparent wonder by the unconscious effect of the mind on the body. The expectation that the stone was going to strike a certain number of times induced an involuntary movement of the hand.[124]

The turquoise seems to have been worn almost exclusively by men at the beginning of the seventeenth century, for De Boot, writing in 1609, said that it was so highly regarded by men that no man considered his hand to be well adorned unless he wore a fine turquoise. Women, however, rarely wore this gem.[125] This custom was much in vogue among the Englishmen who travelled in the Orient, until a score of years ago.

The Persians fully appreciate the beauty and power of this, their national stone, and they have a saying that to escape evil and attain good fortune one must see the reflection of the new moon either on the face of a friend, on a copy of the Koran, or on a turquoise,[126] thus ranking this stone with two most precious things, a friend and the source and warrant of religion. Possibly we should take this proverbial saying to indicate that whoever has a true friend, a copy of the sacred volume or a turquoise will be preserved from harm.

The turquoise of the Los Cerillos mines in New Mexico is rudely extracted by building large fires at the

---

[124] De Boot, "Gemmarum et lapidum historia," Lug. Bat., 1636, pp. 169, 170.

[125] De Boot, l. c., p. 270.

[126] Hendley, "Indian Jewelry," London, 1909, p. 158.

base of the rock until it becomes heated, when cold water is dashed over it, the sharp change of temperature splitting up the rock. Some of the fragmentary material thus secured is worked up in the region into heart-shaped ornaments, or amulets, locally called malacates. The religious veneration with which many of the New Mexico Indians still regard the turquoise was noted by Major Hyde, when he explored the region in 1880, for some Pueblo Indians from Santo Domingo, New Mexico, expressed strong disapproval of his action in extracting turquoise from the old mine, as they looked upon this as a sacred stone which should not pass into the possession of those whose Saviour was not a Montezuma.[127]

The ruins called Los Muertos, situated nine miles from Tempe, Arizona, have furnished a peculiarly interesting amulet or fetish of Zuñi workmanship. This is a seashell which has been coated with black pitch, in which are encrusted turquoises and garnets so disposed in mosaic as to represent clearly enough the figure of a toad, the sacred emblem of the Zuñis.[128]

The sacred character with which this stone was invested is shown by the wealth of turquoise ornaments found in some of the burials, notably in those of Pueblo Bonito, unearthed by Mr. George H. Pepper in 1896.[129] This is one of the Chaco Cañon groups of ruins, in the northwestern part of New Mexico. In one case nearly nine thousand beads and pendants of turquoise were found on or about a single skeleton. There was abun-

---

[127] Kunz, " Gems and Precious Stones of North America," New York, 1890, pp. 61, 62, pl. opposite p. 56.

[128] Kunz, l. c., see pl. 2, fig. A.

[129] Pepper, " The Exploration of a Burial-room in Pueblo Bonito, New Mexico," Putnam Anniversary Volume, New York, 1909, pp. 196–252.

TURQUOISE NECKLACE, THIBET.
Field Museum, Chicago.

dant evidence in the special care bestowed upon the burial that the deceased must have been a man of high rank, and the condition of the skull plainly indicated that he had met a violent death. The 1980 beads found on the breast of the skeleton are believed to have been strung as a necklace, and the position of other masses of these beads renders it probable that they had been used for bracelets or anklets, the strings having decayed and disappeared in the course of time. The most interesting of the turquoise objects are, however, the pendants worked into various forms designed to favor the entrance of some guardian spirit into the stone. In this single burial were found pendants shaped more or less roughly into the forms of a rabbit, a bird, an insect (?), a human foot and a shoe. Around another burial in the same chamber were strewn nearly six thousand turquoise beads and pendants.[130]   In all 24,932 beads were found in these burials.

Another very interesting object from Pueblo Bonito, and one having probably a special ceremonial use and value, is a turquoise basket,—that is to say, a cylindrical basket three inches in diameter and six inches long, originally made of slender splints with a coating of gum in which 1214 small pieces of turquoise have been set. These are very closely set and form a complete mosaic covering for the object. The legends of the Navahos contain allusions to "turquoise jewel baskets," and Mr. Pepper raises the question whether or no this can refer to those made by the Pueblo Indians.[131]

The Apache name for the turquoise is *duklij*, which

---

[130]Pepper, " The Exploration of a Burial-room in Pueblo Bonito, New Mexico," pp. 223, 224.

[131] Pepper, l. c., p. 227.

8

signifies either a green or a blue stone, no distinction being made between the two colors. This stone is highly prized for its talismanic virtues. Indeed the possession of a turquoise was indispensable for a medicine-man, as without it he would not receive proper recognition. That some of the powers of the thunder-stone were ascribed to the turquoise by the tribes appears from the fancy that a man who could go to the end of a rainbow after a storm and search in the damp earth would find a turquoise. One of its supposed powers was to aid the warrior or hunter by assuring the accuracy of his aim, for if a turquoise were affixed to a gun or bow the shot sped from the weapon would go straight to the mark.[132]

A lady prominent in the London world is said to possess the power of restoring to their pristine hue turquoises that have grown pale. According to report, this lady is often called upon to use her peculiar gift by friends whose turquoises have faded.[133] While the improvement supposed to be noted may be more imaginary than real in many cases, there is little doubt that this stone is exceptionally sensitive to the action of certain emanations, and may, at times, be influenced by the wearer's general state of health. The writer believes that a turquoise, like an egg, can never be restored to its original state.

---

[132] Burke, " The Medicine-men of the Apache," Ninth Annual Report of the Bureau of Ethnology, 1887–1888, Washington, 1892, p. 589.

[133] Fernie, " Precious Stones for Curative Use," Bristol, 1907, p. 269.

IV

On the Use of Engraved and Carved Gems as Talismans

THE virtue believed to be inherent in precious stones was thought to gain an added potency when the stone was engraved with some symbol or figure possessing a special sacredness, or denoting and typifying a special quality. This presupposes a considerable development of civilization, since the art of engraving on precious stones offers many mechanical difficulties and thus requires a high degree of artistic and mechanical skill. It is true that the earliest engraved stones, the Babylonian cylinders and the Egyptian scarabs, were both designed to serve an eminently practical purpose as well, namely, that of seals; but in a great number of instances these primitive seals were looked upon as endowed with talismanic power, and were worn on the person as talismans.

The scarab, so highly favored by the Egyptians as an ornamental form, is a representation of the *scarabæus sacer,* the typical genus of the family *Scarabæidæ.* They are usually black, but occasionally show a fine play of metallic colors. After gathering up a clump of dung for the reception of the eggs, the insect rolls this along, using the hind legs to propel it, until the material, at first soft and of irregular form, becomes hardened and almost perfectly round. A curious symbolism induced the Egyptians to find in this beetle an emblem of the world of fatherhood and of man. The round ball wherein the eggs were deposited typified the world, and, as the Egyptians thought that the scarabæi were all males, they especially signified the male principle in generation, becoming types of fatherhood and man. At the same time, as only full-grown beetles were observed, it was believed these creatures represented a regeneration or reincarnation, since it was not realized that the eggs or larval and pupa stages had anything to do with the generation of the beetle. Thus the scarab was used as a symbol of immortality.

While, however, this was the popular view, it seems unlikely that such close observers as were the more cultured Egyptians should have been entirely unfamiliar with the real genesis of the *Scarabæus sacer;* but, in this case also, there would have been no difficulty in finding it emblematic of immortality in the various stages through which it passed. The larval stage might well signify the mortal life; the pupa stage, the intermediate period represented by the mummy, with which the soul was conceived to be vaguely connected, in spite of its wanderings through the nether-world; and, lastly, the fully developed beetle could be regarded as a type of the rebirth into everlasting life, when the purified and perfected soul again animated the original and transfigured form in a mysterious resurrection.

Scarabs are frequently engraved with the hieroglyph ☥ (*anch,* "life") and 𓋹𓊽𓋹 (*ha,* "increase of power").

The emblem of stability 𓊽 (*tet*) is also employed, as well as many others. In addition to these simple symbols, many scarabs bear legends supposed to render them exceptionally luck-bringing. The following are characteristic specimens.[1]

---

[1] From " The Sacred Beetle," by John Ward, London, 1902, Plate VIII, Nos. 46, 58, 89, 275, 276, 446.

maat. ankh neb, "Lord of Truth and Life."

"abounding in graces" (very deeply cut as a seal).

"May thy name be established; mayst thou have a son."

(within ornamental border), "good stability."

ikht neb nefer, "All good things."

(Inlaid). "A good day" (a holiday).

"A mother is a truly good thing" or "Truth is a good Mother."

The scarab, for the Egyptians a type of the rising sun and hence of the renewal of life after death, was copied by the Phœnicians from the Egyptian types and modified in various ways to suit the religious fancies of the various lands to which they bore the products of their art. Much of the original significance of this symbol must have been lost; probably in many cases little was left but a vague idea that an amulet of this form would bring good luck to the wearer and guard from harm.

Funeral scarabs were often made of jasper, amethyst, lapis-lazuli, ruby, or carnelian, with the names of gods, kings, priests, officials, or private persons engraved on the base; occasionally monograms or floral devices were engraved. Sometimes the base of the scarab was heart-shaped and at others the scarab was combined with the "utat," or eye of Horus, and also with the frog, typifying revivification. Set in rings they were placed on the fingers of the dead, or else, wrapped in linen bandages, they rested on the heart of the deceased, a type of the sun which rose each day to renewed life. They were symbols of the resurrection of the body.[2]

---

[2] Budge, "The Mummy," Cambridge, 1894, pp. 234–235.

Some of the Egyptian scarabs were evidently used as talismanic gifts from one friend to another. Two such scarabs are in the collection of the Metropolitan Museum of Art in New York. One bears the inscription "May Ra grant you a happy New Year," the text of the other reading as follows: "May your name be established, may you have a son," and "May your house flourish every day." It is a curious fact that the modern greeting "Happy New Year" was current in Egypt probably three thousand years ago.[3]

On the Egyptian inscribed scarabs used as signets were engraved many of the symbols to which a talismanic virtue was attributed. The uræus serpent, signifying death, is sometimes associated with the knot, the so-called *ankh* symbol, denoting life. Often the hieroglyph for *nub,* gold, appears; this symbol is a necklace with pendant beads, showing that gold beads must have been known in Egypt in the early days when the hieroglyph for gold was first used. All these symbolic figures, of which a great number occur, served to impart to the signet a sacred and auspicious quality which communicated itself to the wearer, and even to the impression made by the seal, this in its turn acquiring a certain magic force. Few of us would be willing to confess to a belief in the innate power of any symbol, but the suggestive power of a symbol is as real to-day as it ever was. Any object that evokes a high thought or serves to emphasize a profound conviction really possesses a kind of magical quality, since it is capable of causing an effect out of all proportion to its intrinsic worth or its material quality.

Many scarabs and signets exist made of the artificial

---

[3] The Metropolitan Museum of Art; the Murch Collection of Egyptian antiquities; supplement to the Bulletin of the Met. Mus. of Art, January, 1910.

cyanus, which was an imitation lapis-lazuli made in
Egypt. This was an alkaline silicate, colored a deep blue
with carbonate of copper. Often a wonderful translucent or opaque blue glass was used. The genuine lapis-
lazuli was also used to a considerable extent for scarabs
and cylinders, in Egypt and Assyria, and gems were also
cut from it in imperial Roman times.[4] A notable instance
of the use of lapis-lazuli in ancient Egypt was as the
material for the image of Truth (*Ma*), which the
Egyptian chief-justice wore on his neck, suspended from
a golden chain.[5]

In Roman times some of the legionaries are said to
have worn rings set with scarabs, for the reason that
this figure was believed to impart great courage and
vigor to the wearer.[6]

The Egyptian amulets of the earliest period, up to the
XII dynasty (circa 2000 B.C.), differ considerably from
those made and worn after the beginning of the XVIII
dynasty (1580 B.C.). Those of the earlier period are not
numerous and present but a small number of types, animal forms or the heads of animals constituting the most
favored models. The precious stone materials are principally carnelian, beryl, and amethyst. After the close of
the so-called Hyksos period, the age during which foreign
kings ruled over Egypt, came the brilliant revival and
development of Egyptian civilization that characterized
the XVIII dynasty. Some of the old forms were entirely
cast aside while others were greatly modified in form and
significance, the animal forms losing much of their fetich-

---

[4] Middleton, " Engraved Gems of Ancient Times," Cambridge,
1891, p. 151.
[5] Diodori Siculi, " Bibliothecæ historicales," ed. Dindorf, Parisiis,
1842, vol. i, p. 65; lib. i, cap. 75.
[6] Æliani, " De animalibus," lib. x, cap. 15.

istic quality and coming to be more and more regarded as images of the multifarious divinities worshipped in this later period. In many cases the animal type was entirely or partially discarded and the amulets figured the conventional types given to the various divinities. However, while some of these images were wholly human, many of them show a human body with an animal head. Various symbolic designs were also favored, one believed to signify the blood of Isis having the form of a knot or tie. A frog fashioned out of lapis-lazuli and having eyes of gold is one of these amulets of the XVIII dynasty or later.

An interesting Egyptian talisman in the Louvre is engraved with a design representing Thothmes II seizing a lion by the tail and raising the animal aloft; at the same time he brandishes in the other hand a club, with which he is about to dash out the lion's brains. The Egyptian word *quen*, "strength," is engraved beneath the design and indicates that the virtue of the talisman was to increase the strength and courage of the wearer, the inscription being a kind of perpetual invocation to the higher powers whose aid was sought.[7]

The children of Israel, when in the desert, were said to have engraved figures on carnelian, "just as seals are engraved."[8] This statement, repeated by many early writers, may perhaps have arisen from an identification of carnelian with the first stone of the breastplate, the *odem*, unquestionably a red stone, and very possibly carnelian. There can be no doubt that this was one of the

---

[7] Hoernes, "Urgeschichte der bildenden Kunst," Wien, 1898, pp. 155, 156.

[8] Konrad v. Megenberg, "Buch der Natur," ed. Pfeiffer, Stuttgart, 1861, p. 448; see also Johannis de Cuba, "Hortus Sanitatis" [Strassburg, 1483], tractatus de lapidibus, cap. xliii.

first stones used for ornamental purposes and for engraving, as a number of specimens have been preserved from early Egyptian times. Because of the cooling and calming effect exercised by carnelian upon the blood, if worn on the neck or on the finger, it was believed to still all angry passions.[9]

A class of amulets even older than the Egyptian scarabs is represented by the engraved Assyrio-Babylonian cylinders. There has been much discussion among scholars as to the original purpose for which these cylinders were made, some holding that they were exclusively employed as seals or signets, while others incline to the belief that many of them were intended only for use as amulets or talismans.

These cylinders are perforated and were worn suspended from the neck or wrist, as is most frequently the case with talismans, and the engraved designs often represent religious or mythological subjects, the accompanying inscription merely consisting of the names of the gods. Cylinders of this type could not have been used as personal signets, and it is quite possible that Dr. Wiedemann is right in supposing that their imprint on a document was considered to impart a certain mystic sanction to the agreement, and render the divinities or spirits accountable for the fulfilment of the contract.[10]

The oldest known form of seal is the cylinder. Babylonian and Assyrian cylinder-seals are known of a date as early as 4000 B.C. From the earliest period until 2500 B.C. they were made of black or green serpentine, conglomerate, diorite, and frequently of the central core of

[9] Marbodei, "De lapidibus," Friburgi, 1531, fol. 19.

[10] Fischer and Wiedemann, "Ueber Babylonische 'Talismane' aus dem hist. Mus. im steierisch-landschaftl. Joanneum zu Graz," Stuttgart, 1881, p. 9.

a large conch shell from the Persian Gulf. From 2500 B.C. to 500 B.C the cylindrical form was prevalent, and the materials include a brick-red ferruginous quartz, red hematite (an iron ore), and chalcedony, a beautiful variety of the last-named stone known as sapphirine being sometimes used. On the cylinders produced from 4000 B.C. to 2500 B.C. the designs most frequently represent animal forms; on those dating from 2500 B.C. to 500 B.C. are generally inscribed five or six rows of cuneiform characters. Up to the last-named date the work was all done by the sapphire point, and not by the wheel, and it is not until the fifth century B.C. that wheel work is apparent in any Babylonian or Assyrian stone-engraving. In the course of the sixth century B.C. the cylindrical seals became less frequent, and the tall cone-like seals came into use.[11]

A new type makes its appearance about the fifth or sixth century B.C., namely, the scaraboid seal introduced from Egypt. From the third century B.C. until the second or third century A.D., the seals became lower and flatter, and the perforation larger, until they sometimes assumed the form of rings; later the ring form becomes general. They are usually hollowed a little in the middle, which gives them the shape and size of the lower short joints of a reed; indeed, it has been suggested that the original seal was rudely patterned after a reed joint. The materials used for these cylinders include lapis-lazuli, very freely used and probably from the Persian mines, jasper, rock-crystals, chalcedony, carnelian, agate, jade, etc.; a hard, black variety of serpentine is perhaps the most common of all the materials used for this purpose.[12]

---

[11] See Ward, " The Seal Cylinders of Western Asia," Carnegie Institution Pub., Washington, D. C., 1910, pp. 1-5.

[12] Ward, l. c., p. 5 and pp. 5-8.

A good example of these talismanic cylinders shows the figure of the god Nebo, seated on a throne and holding a ring in his left hand. Before him are two altars, over which appear, respectively, a star and the crescent moon; in front of the god is the figure of a man in an attitude of adoration. Borsippa, where the cylinder was found, was the special seat of the worship of Nebo, whose name appears in those of the kings Nebuchadnezzar, Nebo-palasser, and Nabonaid. Regarded as the inventor of writing and as the god of learning, Nebo was the lord of the planet Mercury, and this shows a close connection between Babylonian and Græco-Roman ideas in reference to the god associated with that planet. Nebo was also believed to be the orderer of times and seasons, and this character is indicated by the star and the crescent.[13]

The Cretan peasants of to-day set a high value upon certain very ancient seals—dating perhaps from as early as 2500 B.C.—which they find buried in the soil. These seals are inscribed with symbols supposed to represent the prehistoric Cretan form of writing. Of course these inscriptions, which have not yet been deciphered by arch-æologists, are utterly incomprehensible for the peasants, but they undoubtedly serve to render the stones objects of mystery. The peasants call them *galopetræ*, or "milk-stones," and they are supposed to promote the secretion of milk, as was the case with the galactite.[14] The careful preservation of these so-called *galopetræ* by Cretan women has served the purpose of archæological research, as otherwise so large a supply of these very interesting seals would not now be available.

---

[13] Fischer and Wiedemann, "Ueber Babylonische Talismane," Stuttgart, 1881, p. 11. See Pl. I, fig. 3.

[14] A. Evans, in "Journal of Hellenic Studies," vol. xiv (1893), p. 270.

Many engraved stones of the Roman imperial period bore the figures of Serapis and of Isis, the former signifying Time and the latter Earth. On other stones the symbols of the zodiacal signs appear, referring to the natal constellation of the wearer. The astrologers, who derived their lore from the Orient, were consulted by all classes of the Roman people, and it is therefore very

1. ENGRAVED HELIOTROPE.

Head of Serapis surrounded by the twelve Zodiacal symbols. From Gori's "Thesaurus Gemmarum Antiquarum Astriferarum," Florence, 1750. Vol. i, Pl. XVII.

2. ENGRAVED RED JASPER.

Head of Medusa, Museum Cl. Passerii.

natural that the signet, or the ring worn as an amulet, should frequently have been engraved with astrological symbols. These designs were usually engraved on onyxes, carnelians, and similar stones, in Greek and Roman times; but occasionally the emerald was used in this way, and more rarely the ruby or the sapphire. Here the costliness of the material was probably thought to en-

hance the value of the amulet. The emerald ring of
Polycrates must have possessed some other than a purely
artistic value in his eyes, when it could be regarded by
him as the most precious of his possessions.

In Roman times the image of Alexander the Great
was looked upon as possessing magic virtues, and it is
related that when Cornelius Macer gave a splendid ban-
quet in the temple of Hercules, the chief ornament of the
table was an amber cup, in the midst of which was a portrait of Alexander, and around this his whole history
figured in small, finely engraved representations. From
this cup Macer drank to the health of the pontifex and
then ordered that it should be passed around among the
guests, so that each one might gaze upon the image of the
great man. Pollio, relating this, states that it was a
common belief that everything happened fortunately for
those who bore with them Alexander's portrait executed
in gold or silver.[15] Indeed, even among Christians coins
of Alexander were in great favor as amulets, and the
stern John Chrysostom sharply rebukes those who wore
bronze coins of this monarch attached to their heads and
their feet.[16]

Nowhere in the world was the use of amulets so common as in Alexandria, especially in the first centuries
of our era, and the types produced here were scattered
far and wide throughout the Roman world. Amulets
made from various colored stones had been used for
religious purposes in Egypt from the very earliest period
of its history, so that the custom was deeply rooted in
that land. When, therefore, Alexandria was founded in

---

[15] Trebelii Pollionis, De XXX tyrannis, Lipsiæ, p. 295.
[16] Ad illum. catech., Hom. II, 5.

the fourth century B.C., and became a great commercial centre, attracting men of all races and all religions, it is not surprising that the population eagerly adopted the various amulets used by the adherents of the different religions. The result was a combining and confusion of many different types. With the rapid rise and growth of the Christian religion, a new element was introduced. Unquestionably the leading Christian teachers were strongly opposed to such superstitious practices, but the rank and file of the faithful clung to their old fancies.

In the second century the Gnostic heresy gave a new impulse to the fabrication of amulets. This strange eclecticism, resulting from an interweaving of pagan and Christian ideas, with its complicated symbolism, much of which is almost incomprehensible, found expression in the creation of the most bizarre types of amulets, and the magic virtues of the curious designs was enhanced by inscriptions purposely obscure. The incomprehensible always seems to have a mysterious charm for those devoted to the magic arts, and the adepts willingly catered to this taste, so that we can often only guess at the signification of the words and names engraved upon the Gnostic or Basilidian gems. So widespread was their use throughout the Roman Empire, that there were factories entirely devoted to the production of these objects.[17]

Regarding the sacred name Abrasax, which was inscribed on so many Gnostic gems, we read in St. Augustine's treatise De hæres., vi, "Basilides asserted that there were 365 heavens; it was for this reason that he regarded the name Abrasax as sacred and venerable."

---

[17] Krause, "Pyrgoteles," Halle, 1856, pp. 197–8.

1. Gnostic gem, heliotrope, with Abraxas god. Gorlaeus Collection. From the "Abraxas seu Apistopistus" of Macarius (L'Heureux) Antwerp, 1657, Pl. II.

2. Another type; with seven stars.

3. Gnostic gem. Type of Abraxas god and mystic letters I A W. From Gori's "Thesaurus Gemmarum Antiquarum Astriferarum," Florence, 1750, vol. i, Pl. CLXXXIX.

4. Abraxas gem, jasper, mystic letters I A W. From Gorlaeus, "Cabinet de Pierres Gravées," Paris, 1778.

5. Jasper engraved with the symbol of the Agathodaemon Serpent. The type of amulet noted by Galen as that used by the Egyptian king "Nechepsus" (Necho 610–594 B.C.). Original at one time in the collection of Johann Schinkel. From the "Abraxas seu Apistopistus" of Macarius (L'Heureux) Antwerp, 1657, Pl. XVII. See page 385.

According to the Greek notation the letters comprising this name give that number:

$$
\begin{aligned}
a &= 1 \\
\beta &= 2 \\
\rho &= 100 \\
a &= 1 \\
\sigma &= 200 \\
a &= 1 \\
\xi &= 60 \\
\hline
&365
\end{aligned}
$$

It is, however, not unlikely that the 365 days in the solar year are signified; and this enigmatical name might thus be brought into connection with Mithra, the solar divinity, who was worshipped throughout the Persian and Roman empires in the first and second centuries of our era.

A very recondite but ingenious explanation of the Gnostic name Abrasax is given by Harduin in his notes to Pliny's "Natural History." [18] He sees in the first three letters the initials of the three Hebrew words signifying father, son, and spirit (*ab, ben, ruah*), the Triune God; the last four letters are the initials of the Greek words ἀνθρώπους σώζει ἁγίῳ ξύλῳ or " he saves men by the sacred wood " (the cross). This seems rather far-fetched, it must be confessed, and yet to any one familiar with the vagaries of Alexandrine eclecticism, and with the tendency of the time and place to make strange and uncouth combinations of Greek and Hebrew forms, there is nothing inherently improbable in the explanation. Indeed, the Hebrew and Greek words in this composite sen-

---

[18] Caii Plinii Secundi, *Naturalis Historia*, ed. Harduin, Parisiis, 1741, vol. ii, p. 489.

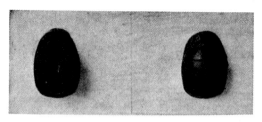

PHOENICIAN SCARAB, WITH ENGRAVED SCORPION. (See page 115.)

ANCIENT BABYLONIAN CYLINDER IMPRESSION, BEARING FIGURES OF
THE GOD NEBO AND A WORSHIPPER, AND SYMBOLS OF
SUN AND MOON.

From Fischer and Wiedemann "Ueber Babylonische Talismane," Stuttgart, 1881, Pl. 1, fig. 3.

A SMALL JADE CELT ENGRAVED WITH GNOSTIC INSCRIPTIONS IN THE
FOURTH CENTURY.

On one side are seven lines of characters, principally consisting of the seven Greek
vowels used to denote the Ineffable Name. On the reverse is cut a laurel branch with 18
leaves, enclosed within each of which are characters expressing the name of one of the personifications of Gnostic theosophy. Brought from Egypt and deposited by its possessor,
General Lefroy, in the Rotunda at Woolwich. Now in the Egyptian Department of the
British Museum. (See page 129.)

tence might have been regarded as typifying the union of the Old and New Testaments, and such an acrostic would certainly have been looked upon as possessing a mystic and supernatural power.

Many explanations have been offered as to the origin and significance of the characteristic figure of the Abrasax god engraved on a number of Gnostic amulets. There seems to be no doubt that this figure was invented by Basilides, chief of the Gnostic sect bearing his name, and who flourished in the early part of the second cen-

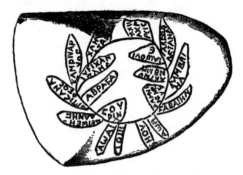

ANTIQUE JADE CELT CONVERTED INTO A GNOSTIC TALISMAN
Enclosed within the outlines of the 18 leaves are as many names of the personifications of Gnostic Theosophy.

tury A.D. While the details of the type as perfected were undoubtedly borrowed from the eclectic symbolism of the Egyptian and western Asiatic world it is almost impossible to conjecture the reasons determining the selection of this particular form.

A jasper engraved with the famous Gnostic symbol was set in the ring worn by Seffrid, Bishop of Chichester (A.D. 1159). This ring was found on the skeleton of the bishop and is now preserved in the treasury of the Cathedral of Chichester. Undoubtedly the curious symbolic figure was given a perfectly orthodox meaning, and, in-

9

deed, it was not really a pagan symbol, as the Gnostics were "indifferent Christians," although their system was a fanciful elaboration of the doctrines of the late Alexandrian school of Greek Philosophy and an adaptation of this to the teachings of Christian tradition. In many cases, however, gems with purely pagan designs were worn by Christians, designs such as Isis with the child Horus, which was taken to be the Virgin Mary with the infant Jesus.

A curious amulet, apparently belonging to the Gnostic variety, and intended to bring success to the owner of a racehorse, is now in the collection of the Metropolitan Museum of Art, in New York. The material is green jasper with red spots. On the obverse the horse is figured with the victor's palm and the name Tiberis; on the reverse appears the vulture-headed figure of the Abraxas god and the characters, "ZACTA IAW BAPIA," which have been translated, "Iao the Destroyer and Creator."[19] Possibly this amulet may have been attached to the horse during his races to insure victory, as we know that amulets of this kind were used in this way.

As illustrating the eclectic character of some of the amulets used in the early Christian centuries, we may note one in the Cabinet de Médailles, in Paris. This has upon the obverse the head of Alexander the Great; on the reverse is a she-ass with her foal, and below this a scorpion and the name Jesus Christ. Another amulet of this class, figured by Vettori,[20] also has the head of Alex-

---

[19] King, Catalogue of Engraved Gems, Metropolitan Museum of Art, p. 81, No. 302, 1885.

[20] Dissert. apol. de quibusdam Alexandri Severi numismat., p. 59. Cited in Dictionnaire de l'arch. chrét., vol. i, Pt. II, Paris, 1907, cols. 1789, 1790, where the amulet is figured.

ander on the obverse, while the reverse bears the Greek monogram of the name Christos.

After the third or fourth century of our era the art of gem-engraving seems to have been lost, or at least to have been very seldom practised, and it is noteworthy in the matter that after this period writers who treat of the virtues of engraved gems as talismans rarely, if ever, use the words ''if you engrave'' such or such a figure on a stone, but write ''if you find'' such a figure.

The figures engraved on precious stones were supposed to have a greater or lesser degree of efficacy in themselves independent of the virtues peculiar to the stone on which they were engraved, and this efficacy depended largely upon the hour, day, or month during which the work was executed. For the influence of the planet, star, or constellation which was in the ascendant was thought to infuse a subtle essence into the stone while the appropriate image was being engraved. However, to exert the maximum power, the virtue of the image must be of the same character as the virtue inherent in the material, and the gem became less potent when this was not the case. Certain images, those symbolizing the zodiacal signs for instance, were looked upon as possessing such power that their peculiar nature impressed itself even upon stones inherently of different quality; others again were only efficacious when engraved on stones the quality of which was in sympathy with them.[21]

Naturally, many of the ancient gems which had been preserved from Greek and Roman times were recognized as being purely products of art, but in medieval and later times the idea of the magic quality of all engraved gems had become so deeply rooted that in many cases a magical

---

[21] Camilli Leonardi, Speculum Lapidum, Venetia, 1502.

character was ascribed to them entirely foreign to the intention of the engraver. Great ingenuity was often displayed in seeking and finding some analogy between the supposed significance of the design and the fancied power of the stone itself. Taking the agate as an illustration, Camillo Leonardo says that its many different varieties had as many different virtues, and he finds in this an explanation of the multiplicity of images engraved on the various kinds of agate, without realizing that the true reason was that this material lent itself more readily to artistic treatment than did many others.

The idea that some special design should be engraved upon a given stone became quite general in the early centuries of our era. The emerald, for instance, according to Damigeron, was to be engraved with a scarab, beneath which was to be a standing figure of Isis. The gem, when completed, was to be pierced longitudinally and worn in a brooch. The fortunate owner of this talisman was then to adorn himself and the members of his family, and, a consecration having been pronounced, he was assured that he would see "the glory of the stone granted it by God." [22] Possibly this may have meant that the stone would become luminous.

A list of these symbolic designs is said to have been given in the "Book of Wings," by Ragiel, one of the curious treatises composed about the thirteenth century under the influence of Hebrew and Greco-Roman tradition. Although it owes its origin to the Hebrew "Book of Raziel," it bears little if any likeness to that work. As will be seen in the following items, the fact that the design is on its appropriate stone is always insisted on:

---

[22] Pitra, "Specilegium Solesmense," Parisiis, 1885, vol. iii, pp. 326, 327.

The beautiful and terrible figure of a dragon. If this is found on a ruby or any other stone of similar nature and virtue, it has the power to augment the goods of this world and makes the wearer joyous and healthy.

The figure of a falcon, if on a topaz, helps to acquire the good-will of kings, princes, and magnates. The image of an astrolabe, if on a sapphire, has power to increase wealth and enables the wearer to predict the future.

The well-formed image of a lion, if engraved on a garnet, will protect and preserve honors and health, cures the wearer of all diseases, brings him honors, and guards him from all perils in travelling.

An ass, if represented on a chrysolite, will give power to prognosticate and predict the future.

The figure of a ram or of a bearded man, on a sapphire, has the power to cure and preserve from many infirmities as well as to free from poison and from all demons. This is a royal image; it confers dignities and honors and exalts the wearer.

A frog, engraved on a beryl, will have the power to reconcile enemies and produce friendship where there was discord.

A camel's head or two goats among myrtles, if on an onyx, has the power to convoke, assemble, and constrain demons; if any one wears it, he will see terrible visions in sleep.

A vulture, if on a chrysolite, has the power to constrain demons and the winds. It controls demons and prevents them from coming together in the place where the gem may be; it also guards against their importunities. The demons obey the wearer.

A bat, represented on a heliotrope or bloodstone, gives the wearer power over demons and helps incantations.

A griffin, imaged on a crystal, produces abundance of milk.

A man richly dressed and with a beautiful object in his hand, engraved on a carnelian, checks the flow of blood and confers honors.

A lion or an archer, on a jasper, gives help against poison and cures from fever.

A man in armor, with bow and arrow, on an iris stone, protects from evil both the wearer and the place where it may be.

A man with a sword in his hand, on a carnelian, preserves the place where it may be from lightning and tempest, and guards the wearer from vices and enchantments.

A bull engraved on a prase is said to give aid against evil spells and to procure the favor of magistrates.

A hoopoo with a tarragon herb before it, represented on a beryl, confers the power to invoke water-spirits and to converse with them, as well as to call up the mighty dead and to obtain answers to questions addressed to them.

A swallow, on a celonite, establishes and preserves peace and concord among men.

A man with his right hand raised aloft, if engraved on a chalcedony, gives success in lawsuits, renders the wearer healthy, gives him safety in his travels and preserves him from all evil chances.

The names of God, on a *ceraunia* stone, have the power to preserve the place where the stone may be from tempests; they also give to the wearer victory over his enemies.

A bear, if engraved on an amethyst, has the virtue of putting demons to flight and defends and preserves the wearer from drunkenness.

A man in armor, graven on a magnet, or loadstone, has the power to aid in incantations and makes the wearer victorious in war.[23]

An Italian manuscript, dating from the fourteenth century, gives the following talismanic gems:

If thou findest a stone on which is graven or figured a man with a goat's head, whoever wears this stone, with God's help, will have great riches and the love of all men and animals.

If a stone be found on which is graven or figured an armed man or the draped figure of a virgin, bound with laurel and having a laurel branch in her hand, this stone is sacred and frees the wearer from all changes and haps of fortune.

When thou findest a stone on which is graven the figure of a man holding a scythe in his hand, a stone like this imparts strength and power to the wearer. Every day adds to his strength, courage and boldness.

Hold dear that stone on which thou shalt find figured or cut the moon or the sun, or both together, for it makes the wearer chaste and guards him from lust.

A jewel to be prized is that stone on which is graven or figured a man with wings having beneath his feet a serpent whose head he

---

[23] Camilli Leonardi, "Speculum Lapidum," Venetia, 1502, ff. lvi–lvii.

holds in his hand. A stone of this kind gives the wearer, by God's help, abundant wealth of knowledge, as well as good health and favor.

Shouldst thou find a stone on which is the figure of a man holding in his right hand a palm branch, this stone, with God's help, renders the wearer victorious in disputes and in battles, and brings him the favor of the great.

Finding the stone called jasper, bearing graven or figured a huntsman, a dog, or a stag, the wearer, with God's help, will have the power to heal one possessed of a devil, or who is insane.

A good stone is that one on which thou shalt find graven or figured a serpent with a raven on its tail. Whoever wears this stone will enjoy high station and be much honored; it also protects from the ill-effects of the heat.[24]

The original meaning of the swastika emblem has been variously explained as a symbol of fire, of the four cardinal points, of water, of the lightning, etc. Still another explanation is given by Hoernes, who inclines to the belief that it is simply a conventionalized representation of the human form, the lower shaft being the two legs joined together, the two horizontal shafts the outstretched arms, and the upper shaft the trunk of the body; the four projections would stand for the feet, the two hands and the head.[25]

The Egyptian crux ansata, the hieroglyphic symbol for "life," and the Phœnician Tau symbol, the "mark" that was to be stamped upon the foreheads of the faithful in Jerusalem (Ezek. ix, 4), and which in Early Christian art was frequently substituted for the usual cross, are both explained by Hoernes in a similar way, and he notes the fact that the swastika symbol does not appear in

---

[24] From an anonymous Italian treatise in a fourteenth century MS. in the author's collection; fol. 40 verso, 41 recto.

[25] Hoernes, " Urgeschichte der bildenden Kunst," Vienna, 1898, p. 338.

Egyptian or Phœnician art, drawing the inference that all three symbols originated in the same form or figure.[26] To all these symbols were attributed talismanic virtues and they were frequently engraved on precious stones.

The so-called "Monogrammatic Cross" was very freely used in work of the fifth century. This is simply a modification of the monogram formed of the first two

MONOGRAM OF THE NAME OF CHRIST ENGRAVED ON AN ONYX GEM.
From the "Cabinet de Pierres Antiques Gravées," of Gorlaeus, Paris, 1778, Pl. XCV.

letters of the name Christ as written in Greek, a device which first appeared after the time of Constantine the Great (d. 337 A.D.). This monogram usually assumed the following form: P, and the "Monogrammatic Cross" was made by changing the position of the Greek X (chi), and making one of its arms serve as the straight stroke of the P (r), thus giving the following form: P.

MOSS AGATE MOCHA STONES, HINDOOSTAN.

A curious amulet to avert the spell of the Evil Eye is an engraved sard showing an eye in the centre, around which are grouped the attributes of the divinities presiding over the days of the week. Sunday, the dies Solis, is represented by a lion; Monday, the dies Lunæ, by a stag; Tuesday, the dies Martis, by a scorpion; Wednesday, the dies Mercurii, by a dog; Thursday, the dies Jovis, by a thunderbolt; Friday, the dies Veneris, by a snake; and Saturday, the dies Saturni, by an owl.[27] In this way the wearer was protected at all times from the evil influence.

Because of its peculiar markings, some of which suggest the form of an eye, malachite was worn in some parts of Italy (e.g., in Bettona) as an amulet to protect the wearer from the spell of the Evil Eye. Such stones were called "peacock-stones," from their resemblance in color and marking to the peacock's tail. The form of these malachite amulets is usually triangular, and they were mounted in silver. It is curious to note, as a proof of the persistence of superstitions, that in an Etruscan tomb at Chiusi there was found a triangular, perforated piece of glass, each angle terminating in an eye formed of glass of various colors.[28]

On many of the amulets fabricated in Italy for protection against the dreaded jettatura, or spell of the Evil Eye, the cock is figured. His image was supposed in ancient times to assure the protection of the sun-god, and his crowing was regarded as an inarticulate hymn of praise to this deity. He was also a type of dauntless courage. All this contributed to make him a defender of

---

[27] King, "The Gnostics and their Remains," London, 1864, p. 238, figure opp. p. 115.

[28] Catalogue de l'Exposition de la Société d'Anthropologie (Exposition de 1900), p. 286.

the weak, especially of women and children, against the wiles of the spirits of darkness.[29] Rostand, in his "Chantecler," has enlarged this conception, and endows the cock with the proud conviction that it is to his matu-

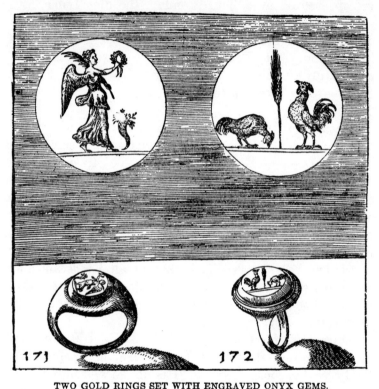

TWO GOLD RINGS SET WITH ENGRAVED ONYX GEMS.

On the right, a Victory; on the left, game-cocks. From the Dactyliotheca, of Gorlaeus, Delft, 1601, Figs. 171, 172.

tinal chant alone that the world owes the daily recurrent phenomenon of the sunrise.

In Palestine the Evil Eye is supposed to be the baleful gift of men who have light-blue eyes, more especially if

---

[29] Elworthy, " The Evil Eye," London, 1895, pp. 353, 354.

they are beardless. Possibly this is the power in which some of our blond and beardless "mashers" repose their trust. As an antidote to the awful influence of these blue-eyed monsters, the Syrian women decorated themselves with blue beads, on the principle *similia similibus curantur*. A maiden with beautiful hair will tie a blue ribbon about it, or wear a blue bead in it, so as to ward off any evil spell cast by the blue eye that might rob her of her fair dower.[30]

It is a well-known fact that many amulets were made in forms suggesting objects offensive to our sense of propriety. These were thought to protect the wearers by denoting the contempt they felt for the evil spirits leagued against them. Some such fancy may have induced the peculiar designs of certain of the jewels alleged to have been pawned in Paris by the ex-Sultan Abdul Hamid for the sum of 1,200,000 francs ($240,000). According to rumor, these pledges must be sold, as the sultan has failed to redeem them, but the designs are so *risqué* that they cannot be offered at public sale; therefore the stones and pearls are to be removed and the gold settings are to be melted and sold as metal.

It is not exclusively characteristic of our commercial and industrial age that the price paid for a work of art should influence the popular estimation of the merits of the work, as appears in an anecdote related by Pliny. An emerald (smaragd), upon which was engraved a figure of Amymone (one of the Danaidæ), having been offered for sale in the Isle of Cyprus, at the price of six golden denarii, Ismenias, a flute-player, gave orders to

[30] Stern, " Medizin, Aborglaube und Geschelechtsleben in der Turkei," Berlin, 1903, vol. i, p. 235.

purchase it. The dealer, however, reduced the price and returned two denarii; upon which Ismenias remarked, "By Hercules! he has done me but a bad turn in this, for the merit of the stone has been greatly impaired by this reduction in price."[31]

A variant of the design directed by Damigeron to be placed on the emerald is recommended in a thirteenth century manuscript, where we read that to fit this stone for use as a talisman, it should be engraved with the form of a scarab, beneath which there should appear a crested paroquet.[32]   According to the same manuscript, a jasper should bear the figure of Mars fully armed, or else that of a virgin wearing a flowing robe and bearing a laurel branch. It should then be "consecrated with perpetual consecration." The mythical author Cethel asserts that the owner of a jasper engraved with the sacred symbol of the cross would be preserved from drowning.[33]

A curious quid pro quo appears in a fifteenth century treatise on gems written in French. Here, in a list of engraved gems suitable for use as amulets, we read, "If you find a dromedary engraved on a stone with hair flowing over its shoulders, this stone will bring peace and concord between man and wife." The original Latin text read, "If you find Andromeda on a stone with hair flowing over her shoulders, etc.[34] The translator's art which could turn Andromeda into a dromedary almost equalled that of the enchantress Circe.

---

[31] Plini, "Historia naturalis," lib xxxvi, cap. 3.

[32] Archæologia, vol. xxx, p. 541, London, 1844; MS. Harl. No. 80, folio 105, recto.

[33] Pitra, " Specilegium Solesmense," Parisiis, 1855, vol. iii, p. 336.

[34] De Mély, in La Grande Encyclopédie. vol. xxv, p. 885, art. Pierres précieuses.

A few even of the early writers were disposed to be sceptical as to the virtues ascribed to these engraved gems, and did not hesitate to assert that the Greek and Roman engravers executed their designs for ornamental purposes rather than to fit the gems for use as talismans. This was undoubtedly true in a large number of cases but nevertheless, as we have seen, many engraved talismans were really cut in the early centuries. As the art of gem engraving was not practised in the Middle Ages, some medieval writers suppose that the engraved talismanic gems current in their time were not works of art, but of nature, and Konrad von Megenberg accepting this view, gave it as his opinion that "God granted these stones their beauty and virtue for the help and comfort of the human race," adding that when he hoped to receive help from them he in no wise denied the grace of God.[35]

Damigeron writes of the sard that, if worn by a woman, it is a good and fortunate stone. It should be engraved with a design showing a grape-vine and ivy intertwined. [36]

A celebrated topaz was that noted by George Agricola as being in the possession of a Neapolitan, Hadrianus Gulielmus.[37] It bore, in ancient Roman characters, the terse and pregnant inscription:

> Natura deficit,
> Fortuna mutatur.
> Deus omnia cernit.

---

[35] Konrad von Megenberg, "Buch der Natur," Stuttgart, 1861, p. 469.

[36] Pitra, "Specilegium Solesmense," Parisiis, 1855, vol. iii, p. 335.

[37] Agricola, "De natura fossilum," lib. vi, Basileæ, 1546, p. 291.

This was very freely rendered by Thomas Nicols as follows: [38]

> Nature by frailty doth dayly waste away.
> Fortune is turn'd and changed every day.
> In all, there is an eye know's no decay.
> Jah sees for aye.

There is in the Imperial Academy at Moscow a turquoise two inches in diameter, inscribed with a text from the Koran in letters of gold. This turquoise was formerly worn by the Shah of Persia as an amulet, and it was valued at 5000 rubles by the jeweller from whose hands it came.[39]

It is well known that Napoleon III was inclined to be superstitious, and there is not, therefore, anything inherently improbable in the report that he left the seal he wore on his watch-chain to his son, the unfortunate Prince Imperial, as a talisman. This seal is said to have borne an inscription in Arabic characters, signifying "The slave Abraham relying on the Merciful One (God)."[40] The talisman lost its virtue on that unlucky day when, in far-off Zululand, the heir to so many hopes was cut off in the first flush of early manhood (see page 64).

---

[38] Nicols, "Faithful Lapidary," London, 1659, p. 107.

[39] Kluge, "Edelsteinkunde," Leipsic, 1860, p. 366.

[40] Fernie, "Precious Stones for Curative Wear," Bristol, 1907, p. 109.

V

⚙️n ⚙️minous and Luminous Stones

THE OPAL

Mother.   Come, let me place a charm upon thy brow,
           And may good spirits grant, that never care
           Approach, to trace a single furrow there!
Daughter. Thy love, my mother, better far than charm,
           Shall shield thy child—and yet this wondrous gem[1]
           Looks as though some strange influence it had won
           From the bright skies—for every rainbow hue
           Shoots quivering through its depths in changeful gleams,
           Like the mild lightnings of a summer eve.
Mother.   Even so doth love pervade a mother's heart;
           Thus, ever active, looks through her fond eyes.[2]

THERE can be little doubt that much of the modern superstition regarding the supposed unlucky quality of the opal owes its origin to a careless reading of Sir Walter Scott's novel, "Anne of Geierstein."[3] The wonderful tale therein related of the Lady Hermione, a sort of enchanted princess, who came no one knew whence and always wore a dazzling opal in her hair, contains nothing to indicate that Scott really meant to represent the opal as unlucky. Lady Hermione's gem was an enchanted stone just as its owner was a product of

---

[1] The opal is said to preserve its wearer from disease; and hence, in the East, is much used in the form of amulets.

[2] From "Gems of Beauty," by the Countess of Blessington, London, 1836.

[3] Sir Walter Scott, "Novels," The Janson Society, New York, 1907, vol. xxiii, pp. 126–138.

enchantment, and its peculiarities depended entirely upon its mysterious character, which might equally well have been attributed to a diamond, a ruby, or a sapphire. The life of the stone was bound up with the life of Hermione; it sparkled when she was gay, it shot out red gleams when she was angry; and when a few drops of holy water were sprinkled over it, they quenched its radiance. Hermione fell into a swoon, was carried to her chamber, and the next day nothing but a small heap of ashes remained on the bed whereon she had been laid. The spell was broken and the enchantment dissolved. All that can have determined the selection of the opal rather than any other precious stone is the fact of its wonderful play of color and its sensitiveness to moisture. Hence we are perfectly justified in returning to the older belief of the manifold virtues of the opal, only remembering that this gem is a little more fragile than many others and should be more carefully handled and guarded.

The opal, October's gem, recalls in its wonderful and varied play of color the glories of a bright October day in the country, when earth and sky vie with each other in brilliancy and the eye is fairly dazzled with the bewildering variety of color.

It rarely happens that Pliny gives any information as to particular jewels, almost all his notices of precious stones being confined to descriptions of their form and color, and data regarding what was popularly believed as to their talismanic or therapeutic power. In the case of the *opalus*, however, he writes as follows: ''There exists to-day a gem of this kind, on account of which the senator Nonius was proscribed by Antony. Seeking safety in flight, he took with him of all his possessions this ring alone, which it is certain, was valued at

2,000,000 sesterces ($80,000).''⁴ The stone was ''as large as a hazel-nut.''

This ''opal of Nonius'' would be the great historic opal if we had any assurance that it was really the stone to which we now give this name. As, however, the principal European source of supply in Hungary does not appear to have been available in classic times to the Romans, and as opals are not found in the places whence, according to Pliny, the *opalus* was derived, we are almost forced to the conclusion that he had some other stone in mind when he gave his eloquent description of the *opalus*. And yet, in spite of all this, Pliny's words so well describe the beauties of a fine opal that it is difficult to determine what other stone he could have meant. For it can well be said of opals that ''There is in them a softer fire than in the carbuncle, there is the brilliant purple of the amethyst; there is the sea-green of the emerald—all shining together in incredible union. Some by their refulgent splendor rival the colors of the painters, others the flame of burning sulphur or of fire quickened by oil.''⁵ Possibly some brilliant varieties of iridescent quartz— ''iris'' quartz, possessing an internal fracture, displays with great brilliancy all the colors of the rainbow, sparkling with wonderful clearness in its field of transparent mineral—might excite the admiration of one who had never seen an opal. Referring again to these quartz crystals, they are often cut so as to form a dome of quartz and are even used as distinct jewels. The fact that Pliny could praise the Indian imitations of the *opalus* in glass, and could state that this stone was more successfully imitated than any other, is an almost de-

---

⁴ Plinii, ''Naturalis historia,'' lib. xxxvii, cap. 6.
⁵ Plinii, l. c.

10

cisive argument against identifying the *opalus* with an opal, for it is well known that no stone is more difficult to imitate.

About the middle of the eighteenth century, a peasant found a brilliant precious stone in some old ruins at Alexandria, Egypt. This stone was set in a ring. It was as large as a hazel-nut and is said to have been an opal cut *en cabochon*. According to the report, it was eventually taken to Constantinople, where it was estimated to be worth "several thousand ducats." [6] The description given of this gem, its apparent antiquity, and the high value set upon it have contributed to induce many to conjecture that it was the celebrated "opal of Nonius." Of course this was nothing but a romantic fancy. It is also quite certain that an opal would scarcely hold its play of color or compactness for twenty centuries, for most opals lose their water—slowly perhaps, but surely—within a lesser space of time. Even the finest Hungarian opals show some loss of life and color within a century or even less, and some transparent Mexican opals lose their color and are filled with flaws within a few years' time.

The Edda tells of a sacred stone called the yarkastein, which the clever smith Volöndr (the Scandinavian Vulcan) formed from the eyes of children. Grimm conjectures that this name designates a round, milk-white opal. Certainly the opal was often called *ophthalmios,* or eyestone, in the Middle Ages, and it was a common idea that the image of a boy or girl could be seen in the pupil of the eye.

Albertus Magnus describes under the name *orphanus*

---

[6] Hesselquist, " Voyages and Travels in the Levant," English trans., London, 1766, pp. 273, 274.

a stone which was set in the imperial crown of the Holy Roman Empire. This gem is believed to have been a splendid opal, and Albertus describes it as follows:

The orphanus is a stone which is in the crown of the Roman Emperor, and none like it has ever been seen; for this very reason it is called orphanus. It is of a subtle vinous tinge, and its hue is as

THE "ORPHANUS JEWEL" IN THE GERMAN IMPERIAL CROWN.
From the "Hortus Sanitatis" of Johannis de Cuba [Strassburg, Jean Pryss, ca. 1483]; De lapidibus, cap. xcii. Author's library.

though pure white snow flashed and sparkled with the color of bright, ruddy wine, and was overcome by this radiance. It is a translucent stone, and there is a tradition that formerly it shone in the night-time; but now, in our age, it does not sparkle in the dark. It is said to guard the regal honor.[7]

---

[7] Alberti Magni, Opera Omnia, ed. Borgnet, Parisiis, 1890, vol. v, p. 42.

Evidently this imperial gem was regarded as *sui generis,* for Albertus has just described the *ophthalmus lapis,* a name frequently bestowed upon the opal in medieval times, reciting the virtues usually ascribed to the opal for the cure of diseases of the eye, and the magic power of the stone to render its wearer invisible, wherefore it was denominated *patronus furum,* or "patron of thieves."

In the Middle Ages the opal mines of Cernowitz, in Hungary, were very actively exploited, and at the opening of the fifteenth century more than three hundred men are said to have been employed here in the search for opals.   At that time, and for many centuries after, no breath of suspicion ever tarnished the fame of the opal as not only a thing of rare beauty, but also a talisman of the first rank.   We are told that blond maidens valued nothing more highly than necklaces of opals, for while they wore these ornaments their hair was sure to guard its beautiful color.   The latter superstitions probably arose from the frangibility of the stone and its occasional loss of fire.

From the earliest times the baleful influence of the Evil Eye has struck terror into the souls of the ignorant and superstitious.   It is believed by some that the name "opal"—written "ophal" in the time of Queen Elizabeth—was derived from *ophthalmos,* the eye, or *ophthalmius,* pertaining to the eye, and that hence the foolish superstition regarding the ill luck of the opal had some connection with the belief in the Evil Eye.   However, this is altogether incorrect, since the stone called *ophthalmius* by early writers, and which seems to have been the opalus of the ancients and our opal, was believed to have a wonderfully beneficial effect upon the sight, and if it was thought to render the wearer invisible, this was only an added virtue of the stone.

The eye-agates were sometimes used to form the eyes of idols. At a later period some of these "agate-eyes" were removed from the statues and cut with a glyptic subject on the lower side. Some of the most interesting antique gems are of this kind. In Aleppo (and elsewhere in the East) there is a certain type of sore known as the "Aleppo button" or "Aleppo boil." The boil frequently does not appear for a long period after infection has taken place. It often appears as a swelling surrounded by a white ring, and there is a belief among the natives that there are "Aleppo stones," these being the so-called "eye-agates" frequently produced by cutting a three-layer, naturally pale yellow or pale gray agate, with intervening white zones in such a way that it looks like an eye or a double-eye, and such stones are used in alleviation of the Aleppo sore. What beneficial influence they may have is due to the fact that the agate is cold and furnishes a little relief for the time.

This "Aleppo boil" or "Oriental sore" so prevalent in many parts of western Asia, is produced, according to the best authorities, by a pathogenic organism *Leishmania tropica* (Wright) 1903. As to the means by which this organism is introduced into the human subject nothing very definite is known, but mosquitoes or *Phlebotomus* have been suggested as possible transmitting agencies.[8]

The eye of some invisible monster, the eye of the dragon, the eye of the serpent, were all regarded as possessed of malign power. It is well known that in the East Indies a peacock's feather is thought to bring ill-luck,

---

[8] Communication of Dr. Frederick Knab, citing Castellani and Chalmers, "Manual of Tropical Medicine," 1910.

the eye in the feather being the baleful point. Even in our own time, and among those for whom this primitive superstition has no terrors, the humorous use of the idea—as shown, for instance, in the "Dick Dead-Eye" of Gilbert and Sullivan's "Pinafore"—proves that the Evil Eye is familiar to our thoughts. For this reason, stones such as those which have been named the cat's-eye, the tiger's-eye, or the oculus Beli, always possess a certain strange interest.

One of the earliest descriptions of the opal in English is that written in the reign of Queen Elizabeth by Dr. Stephen Batman (d. 1584). While the passage is essentially a translation from the "De proprietatibus rerum," of Bartolomæus Anglicus, the English version is interesting in itself as showing what was accepted by English readers of the time regarding the virtues of the opal. There is, of course, no trace of the foolish modern superstition touching the ominous quality of this beautiful gem. Batman writes: [9]

> Optallio is called Oppalus also, and is a stone distinguished with colors of divers precious stones, as *Isid.* saith. . . . This stone breedeth onely in *Inde* and is deemed to have as many virtues, as hiewes and colours. Of this *Optallius* it is said in Lapidario, that this *Optallius* keepeth and saveth his eyen that beareth it, cleere and sharp and without griefe, and dimmeth other men's eyen that be about, with a maner clowde, and smiteth them with a maner blindnesse, that is called *Amentia*, so that they may not see neither take heede what is done before their eyen. Therefore it is said that it is the most sure patron of theeves.

The opal seems to have appealed to Shakespeare as a fit emblem of inconstancy, for in "Twelfth Night" he makes the clown say to the Duke: [10]

---

[9] Batman, "Uppon Bartholome," London, 1582, p. 264, lib. xvi, cap. 73.

[10] Shakespeare, "Twelfth Night," Act ii, Sc. 4.

Now the melancholy God protect thee, and the Tailor make thy garment of changeable taffeta, for thy mind is very opal.

That the beauty of the opal was fully appreciated in the sixteenth century is shown by the words of Cardano, who states that he once bought one of these stones for fifteen gold crowns and found as much pleasure in its possession as he did in that of a diamond that had cost him five hundred crowns.[11] Although superstitious beliefs were rather the rule than the exception in Cardano's time, none of the silly fancies regarding the ominous quality of the opal were then current. It was reserved for the nineteenth century to develop these altogether unreasonable—and indeed almost inexplicable— superstitions. The ownership of so fair an object as a fine opal must certainly be a source of pleasure, and hence add to the good fortune of the owner.

Although opal has been considered by some a stone of misfortune, black opal is regarded as an exceptionally lucky stone. Formerly black opals were artificially made by dipping the light-colored stone into ink, or by allowing burnt oil to enter cracks in the stone produced by heating. About the year 1900, however, a number of deposits of natural black opals were found in the White Cliff region of New South Wales, whence exceedingly beautiful gems have been secured, with wonderful flames of green, red, and blue in a black field. Some of these have sold for $1000 and even for a higher price, the smaller ones bringing from a few dollars upward each. It has been claimed that $2,000,000 worth have been sold from New South Wales. A remarkable example is figured on the frontispiece of this volume. The late F. Marion Crawford was a great admirer of this strangely beautiful variety of opal.

That ill-luck and good-luck are relative terms is shown

[11] Cardani, "De subtilitate," Basileæ, 1560, p. 445.

as published of an opal by Paris newspapers. A shop-girl, plainly clad, in crossing the Place de l'Opéra, when the street traffic was at its greatest, stopped at one of the "refuges" halfway across the street. To the girl's great surprise, an elegantly attired lady standing there slipped an opal ring from her finger and gave it to the girl, who took it to a jeweller's shop to sell it. Here she was arrested on suspicion of having stolen it. The magistrate before whom she appeared was inclined to believe her story and ordered a "personal" in a widely read journal asking the lady to clear the girl of the charge. A titled lady presented herself, substantiating the girl's statement. She feared ill-luck would befall her if she wore or kept the ring, which was returned to the shopgirl.

A possible explanation of the superstitious dread the opal used to excite some time ago may be found in the fact that lapidaries and gem-setters to whom opals were entrusted were sometimes so unfortunate as to fracture them in the process of cutting or setting. This was frequently due to no fault on the part of the cutters or setters, but was owing to the natural brittleness of the opal. As such workmen are responsible to the owners for any injury to the gems, they would soon acquire a prejudice against opals, and would come to regard them as unlucky stones. Very widespread superstitions have no better foundation than this, for the original cause, sometimes a quite rational one, is soon lost sight of and popular fantasy suggests something entirely different and better calculated to appeal to the imagination.

The belief that the diamond fractured the teeth if it were put in the mouth, and ruptured the intestines if it were swallowed, already appears in pseudo-Aristotle,[12]

---

[12] Rose, " Aristoteles De lapidibus und Arnoldus Saxo," in Zeitschr. für D. Alt., New Series, vol. vi, p. 391. See also Avicenna, " Liber canonis," Basileæ, 1556, p. 182, lib. ii, Tract. ii, cap. 20.

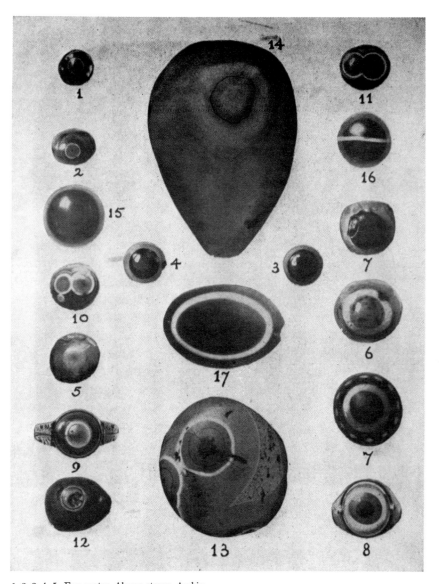

1, 2, 3, 4, 5. Eye agates, Aleppo stones, Arabia.
6 and 7. Antique eye agates, with double zone.
8 and 9. Aleppo stones set in rings.
10 and 11. Double eye agates, Aleppo stones, Arabia.
12. Natural pebble, showing eye from Isle Royal, Lake Superior.
13 and 14. Natural agates with eye-like effect, East Indian. Had been used as votive charms.
15. Eye agate, Brazil.
16. Agate called Oriental agate, eye effect, from Brazil.
17. Ancient eye of idol, agate variety sardonyx. Had been pierced lengthwise and worn as a charm on the arm. East Indian.

and can therefore be dated back to the ninth and perhaps to the seventh century. This fancy evidently owes its origin to the fact that the diamond, because of its hardness, was used to cut all other stones, and the idea of its destructive quality was strengthened by the old legends regarding the venomous serpents which guarded the place where it was found. Hence the firm conviction that it would bring death to any one who swallowed it.

According to Garcias ab Orta (1563), the diamond was not used for medicinal purposes in the India of his time, except when injected into the bladder to break up vesical calculi. He notes, however, the prevalent belief that diamonds, or diamond dust, when taken internally, worked as a poison. As a proof of the falsity of this belief, Garcias adduces the fact that the slaves who worked in the diamond mines often swallowed diamonds to conceal them, and never experienced any ill effects, the stones being recovered in a natural way. The same author notes the case of a man who suffered from chronic dysentery and whose wife had for a long time administered to him doses of diamond dust. If this did not help him, neither did it injure him; finally, by the advice of the doctors, this strange treatment was abandoned. The man eventually died of his disease, but many days after the doses of diamond dust had been discontinued.[13]

The Hindus believed that a flawed diamond, or one containing specks or spots, was so unlucky that it could even deprive Indra of his highest heaven. The original shape of the stone was also considered of great importance, more especially in early times, when but few, if any, diamonds, were cut. A triangular stone was said to cause

---

[13] Garcias ab Orta, "Aromatum historia" (Lat. version by Clusius). Antverpiæ, 1579, p. 172. The Portuguese original was published in Goa, in 1563.

quarrels, a square diamond inspired the wearer with vague terrors; a five-cornered stone had the worst effect of all, for it brought death; only the six-cornered diamond was productive of good.[14]

The Turkish sultan Bejazet II (1447–1512) is said to have been done to death by a dose of pulverized diamond administered to him by his son Selim, who mixed the diamond dust with the sultan's food.[15] It is also related that the disciples of Paracelsus (1493–1541) spread the report that he died from the effects of a dose of diamond dust. Ambrosius [16] conjectures that this was only an excuse to explain the demise of the master in the prime of life—he was but forty-eight years old at the time of his death—although he had promised long life to all who made use of his medicaments.

While Benvenuto Cellini (1500–1571), the unrivalled goldsmith, was imprisoned in Rome, in 1538, he strongly suspected that his enemies were seeking to poison him by tampering with his food. Cellini shared the belief of his contemporaries that there was no more deadly poison than diamond dust. One day, while eating his noonday meal, he felt something grate between his teeth. He paid no particular attention to this, but when he had finished eating his eye was caught by some bright particles on the plate. Picking up one of these and examining it carefully, he was terrified to find what he supposed to be a diamond splinter, and he straightway gave himself up for lost, thinking that he had swallowed a quantity of diamond dust. He prayed to God for an hour and finally

---

[14] Surindro Mohun Tagore, "Mani Mālá," Pt. I, Calcutta, 1879, pp. 122, 125.

[15] Justi Lepsii, "De fraude et vi," cap. v, §8; cited in Pindar, "De adamante," Berolini, 1829, p. 58.

[16] Aldrovandi, "Museum metallicum," Bononiæ, 1648, p. 949.

became reconciled to the thought of dying, but suddenly it occurred to him that he had not tested the hardness of the fragment he had found in his food. He immediately took the splinter and tried to crush it between his knife and the stone window-sill; to his joy the attempt succeeded, and he became convinced that what he had swallowed was not diamond dust. Later, after his release, Cellini learned that an enemy had given a diamond to a certain Lione Aretino, a gem-cutter, instructing him to grind it up so that the dust could be placed in Cellini's food. The gem-cutter was very poor and the diamond was worth a hundred scudi, so the man yielded to temptation and substituted a citrine for the diamond. To this circumstance alone did Cellini attribute his escape from death.[17]

In England, more than seventy years after Cellini's experience, diamond dust was selected as a poison to do away with a luckless prisoner. Sir Thomas Overbury had incurred the bitter animosity of the Countess of Essex, because he opposed her marriage with the favorite of James I, Robert Carr, Viscount Somerset, whom he had befriended and whose career he had furthered. The marriage took place, however, and, in 1613, Overbury was imprisoned in the Tower, through the machinations of the countess. She then sought the aid of one James Franklin, an apothecary, directing him to concoct a slow and deadly poison, which should be mixed with Overbury's food. In the minutes of Franklin's confession, he is said to have stated that the countess asked him what he thought of white arsenic. His reply was that this poison would prove too violent. "What say you (quoth she) to powder of diamonds?" He answered, "I know

---

[17] Vita di Benvenuto Cellini, ed. Carpani, Milano, 1806, p. 445.

not the nature of that.'' She said that he was a fool, and gave him pieces of gold, and bade him buy some of that powder for her. It appears, however, from the testimony, that a number of ingredients were employed, quite probably small doses of mercury, cantharides, etc., as well as the baleful diamond dust. Poor Overbury lingered on for more than three months, but was finally put out of his misery by a clyster of corrosive sublimate.[18]

As a proof of the deadly effects caused by the diamond, the Portuguese Zacutus relates the case of a merchant's servant who surreptitiously swallowed three rough diamonds belonging to his master. On the following day this man was seized with violent abdominal pains, all the remedies administered to him were without effect, and he soon died from the extensive internal ulceration produced by the sharp edges of the diamonds.[19]

This old fancy that diamonds or diamond dust had deadly effects when swallowed is pretty well exploded by this time, little or no confirmation being afforded by the instances cited in the matter. However, quite recently it has been shown that swallowing a diamond can prove fatal to a fowl. While a prize-winning cockerel was being fondled by his proud owner, it spied a flashing diamond set in a ring on his hand, and immediately pecked out the stone and swallowed it. Not long after, the fowl died—not, however, because it was poisoned by the diamond, but because it was chloroformed to insure the speedy recovery of the stone.

An old English ballad, treating of the loves of Hind Horn and Maid Rimnild, recounts that when Hind Horn,

---

[18] Amos, " The Great Oyer of Poisoning," London, 1846, pp. 336 sqq.

[19] Aldrovandi, " Museum metallicum," Bononiæ, 1648, p. 949.

who loved and was beloved by the king's daughter, went
to sea to escape the wrath of the king, the princess gave
him a ring set with seven diamonds. We are told that
when far from home:

> One day he looked his ring upon
> He saw the diamond pale and wan.

Hereupon, he hastened back, for the paleness of the
stone was a sign the loved one was unfaithful to him.
On his return, he succeeded in preventing her marriage
to another, and everything ended happily.[20]

In a fourteenth century MS. of the Old English ro-
mance upon which the ballad is founded, the stone in the
ring is not named; in giving it Rimnild says: [21]

> Loke thou forsake it for no thing;
> The ston it is well trewe.
> When the ston wexeth wan
> Than chaungeth the thought of thi leman,

> Take than a newe.
> When the ston wexeth rede,
> Than have Y lorn mi maidenhed,
> Oghaines [22] the untrewe.

In this older form of the tale, the stone either grows
pale or red as a sign of misfortune. It is interesting to
note that Epiphanius, writing a thousand years earlier,
states that the *adamas* of the high-priest grew red as a
presage of bloodshed and defeat for the Jews.

Regarding the old fancy that a serpent could not look

---

[20] Child, " The English and Scottish Popular Ballads," Boston,
1882–96, vol. i, pp. 187 sqq.

[21] Child, l. c.

[22] Against thee.

upon an emerald without losing its sight, the Arabian gem dealer, Ahmed Teifashi, in 1242 writes as follows: [23]

After having read in learned books of this peculiarity of the emerald, I tested it by my own experiment and found the statements exact. It chanced that I had in my possession a fine emerald of the *zabâbi* variety, and with this I decided to make the experiment on the eyes of a viper. Therefore, having made a bargain with a snake-charmer to procure me some vipers, as soon as I received them I selected one and placed it in a vessel. This being done, I took a stick of wood, attached to the end a piece of wax, and embedded my emerald in this. I then brought the emerald near to the viper's eyes. The reptile was strong and vigorous, and even raised its head out of the vessel, but as soon as I approached the emerald to its eyes, I heard a slight crepitation and saw that the eyes were protruding and dissolving into a humor. After this the viper was dazed and confused; I had expected that it would spring from the vessel, but it moved uneasily hither and thither, without knowing which way to turn; all its agility was lost, and its restless movements soon ceased.

Wolfgang Gabelchover, in his commentary on the sixth book of the treatise "De Gemmis," by Andrea Baccio, gives the following account of a strange and tragic experience in regard to a ruby: [24]

It is worthy of note that the true Oriental ruby, by frequent changes of color and by growing obscurity, announces to the wearer some impending misfortune or calamity; and the obscurity and opacity is greater or less according to the extent of the coming ill-fortune. Alas! that what I had often heard proclaimed by learned men, I should myself experience; for as, on the fifth of December, 1600, I was travelling from Stuttgart to Calw with my beloved wife Catherine Adelmann of pious memory, I plainly observed in the course of the journey that a very beautiful ruby which she had given me, and which I wore on my hand, set in a gold ring, once and again lost

---

[23] Ravii, " Specimen Arabicum," Trajecti ad Rhenum, 1784, pp. 97, 98.

[24] Andreæ Baccii, " De gemmis et lapidibus pretiosis," Latin trans. by Wolfgang Gabelchover, Francofurti, 1603, pp. 63, 64.

its splendid coloring and became obscure, changing its brightness for a dark hue. This dark hue continued not for one or two days only, but so long that I was greatly terrified, and, removing the ring from my finger, concealed it in a case. Wherefore, I repeatedly warned my wife that some great calamity was impending either for her or for myself, the which I inferred from the change and variation of the ruby. Nor was I deceived, for within a few days she was seized with a dangerous illness, which resulted in her death.

A story explaining one at least of these supposedly ominous changes of color in precious stones, is given by Johann Jacob Spener, who states that it was told him by a trustworthy informant: [25]

There was a jeweller, expert, prudent, and rich, three essential qualities in a jeweller. One day, after having washed his hands, this man sat at a table, when, glancing at a ruby ring he wore on his finger, he remarked that the stone, which usually delighted the eye with its splendor, had lost its brilliancy and become dull. Since he believed what others had related to him, he was firmly persuaded that some misfortune threatened him, and, having removed the ring from his finger, he placed it in its case. A fortnight later, one of this man's sons died of varioloid. Reminded by this event of the phenomenon observed in the ruby, the jeweller took it from the case and found, on examination, that it had regained its pristine brilliancy. This fac' confirmed him in his belief in the ominous quality of the stone. Once more, shortly after washing his hands, he remarked anew that the splendor of the ruby was dimmed, and he again fell a prey to anxiety, lest some fresh misfortune was impending. Since, however, his apprehensions proved vain and no untoward event happened, he investigated the matter carefully, and discovered that the obscuration of the color was due to a drop of water which had penetrated between the ruby and the foil, as the jewellers call it, and that the former brilliancy returned when the water had evaporated.

The ominous character of the onyx is especially noted in Arabic tradition, as is shown by the Arabic name for the stone, *el jaza*, "sadness." The following passage

---

[25] " De gemmis errores vulgares," Lipsiæ, 1688, sect. ii, §12.

from pseudo-Aristotle offers an illustration of the strength of this prejudice against the onyx, which was said to come from China and the Magreb: [26]

Those who are in the land of China fear this stone so much that they dread to go into the mines where it occurs; hence none but slaves and menials, who have no other means of gaining a livelihood, take the stone from the mines. When it has been extracted, it is carried out of the country and sold in other lands. Those men of the Magreb also who are gifted with any wisdom will not wear an onyx or place it in their treasuries. Indeed, no one is willing to wear it, unless he be bereft of his senses; for whosoever wears it, either set in a ring or in any other way, will have fearful dreams and be tormented by a multitude of doubts and apprehensions; he will also have many disputes and lawsuits. Lastly, whoever keeps an onyx in his house, or places it in a vessel, or puts it in food or drink, will suffer loss of energy and capacity.

An ominous character was attributed to the red coral, especially the more highly colored varieties. If worn so that the substance came in direct contact with the skin, it was asserted that the color would pale, the coral also losing its brightness if the wearer became ill, or even if he were only threatened with severe illness. The same effect was said to be induced if some deadly poison had been taken. Cardano writes that he more than once observed this phenomenon, and he thinks that in these cases, where the wearer was not yet attacked by disease, its threatening "vapor," though not strong enough to provoke decided symptoms in the human body, was sufficiently powerful to offset the more delicate and subtle essence of the mineral substance. Of course, for us the mineral would be much less sensitive than flesh and blood, but the sixteenth century writers, and to a still greater

---

[26] Rose, Aristoteles De lapidibus and Arnoldus Saxo, Zeitschr. für D. Alt., New Series, vol. vi, 1875, pp. 360, 361.

degree those of an earlier time, attributed to stones not only life in a general way, but old age, disease, and death, in a very positive sense.[27]

Rabbinical tradition tells of a wonderful luminous stone placed by Noah in the Ark. This stone shone more brilliantly by day than by night, and served to distinguish the day from the night when, during the flood, neither sun nor moon could be seen.[28]   According to another Jewish legend, Abraham is said to have built a city for the six sons Hagar bore to him. The wall with which this city was surrounded was so lofty that the light of the sun was cut off, and to offset this Abraham gave to his sons enormous precious stones and pearls. These exceeded the sun in brightness, and will be used in the time of the Messiah.[29]

Ælian relates the following tale of a luminous stone. A woman of Tarentum, named Heracleis, who was a pattern of the domestic virtues, lost her husband and mourned sincerely for him. Her grief made her compassionate, for when a young stork just learning to fly lost its strength and fell to the ground before her, Heracleis picked up the helpless bird and tended it carefully until its strength returned and it was able to fly away. A year later, when the woman was outside the house enjoying the bright warm sunshine, she saw a stork flying toward her. As the bird passed over her head, it let fall a precious stone into her lap. Heracleis took the

---

[27] Cardani, " De subtilitate," Basileæ, 1554, lib. vii, pp. 191, 205.

[28] Ginsburg, "Legends of the Jews," Eng. trans., Phila., 1909, vol. i, p. 162. See also Levy, "Dictionary of the Targumim," etc., New York and London, 1903, vol. ii, p. 836, s. v. מִרְנָלִית· Pirke d'R. El., ch. xxiii.

[29] Ginsburg, l. c., p. 298.

11

stone with her into the house, feeling by an infallible in-
stinct that the stork which had dropped it was the one she
had cared for in the previous year. During the night she
woke up, and was astonished to see that the room was
lighted up as though by many torches, the radiance proceeding from the stone bestowed by the stork as a proof
of its gratitude.[30]

In German, the stone called *Donnerkeil* (thunderbolt)
has several synonyms; among these is *Storchstein*
("stork-stone"). It is evident that the stone of Heracleis
was identical with the precious and brilliant variety of
cerauniæ mentioned by Pliny, "which drew to themselves
the radiance of the stars." The flashing and ruddy light
of the ruby suggested an igneous origin, and induced the
belief that rubies were generated by a fire from heaven,—
in other words, by the lightning flash.[31]

The analogy between the flame of a lamp or the glow
of a burning coal and the radiance of a ruby, suggested
some of the names given to this stone, or those resembling
it in color, as, for instance, the Greek *anthrax* and the
Latin *carbunculus* and *lychnis*. Probably the fancy that
such stones were luminous in the dark was nothing more
than the logical result of the quasi-identification of them
with fire in some of its manifestations. Still, it is a well-
known fact that some stones possess a high degree of
phosphorescence. This circumstance must have been
observed by chance, and may have had something to do
with the legends of luminous stones, although this peculiarity is not characteristic of the ruby.

According to Pliny, the lychnis, perhaps a spinel, was

---

[30] Claudii Æliani, " De animalium natura," lib. viii, cap. 22, ed.
Gesner, Tiguri, 1568, pp. 182, 183.

[31] Grimm, " Wörterbuch," vol. ii, col. 1244.

so called *a lucernarum accensu* (from the lighting, or the light, of lamps). The author of the poem ''Lithica'' says that the diamond (*adamas*), like the crystal, when placed on an altar, sent forth a flame without the aid of fire.[32] If this did not refer to the use of rock-crystal as a burning-glass, we might see in the passage an indication that the phosphorescence of the diamond had already been noted before the second or third century of our era.

From the Lydian river Tmolus a marvellous stone was taken which was said to change color four times a day. This surpasses the properties of the ''saphire merveilleux'' which changed its hue at night. Only innocent young girls could find the Lydian stone, and while they wore it they were defended from outrage.[33] Is it possible that the ancient writer intended to hint at the proverbial fickleness of woman, when stating that this changeable stone could only be discovered by one of the fair sex?

The temple of the Syrian goddess Astarte contained an image of this divinity crowned with a diadem in which was set a luminous stone. Such was the splendor of the light emitted by this gem that the whole sanctuary was lighted up as though with a myriad of lamps. Indeed, the stone itself bore the name *lychnos* (''lamp''). In the daytime this light was fainter, but was still very noticeable, as a fiery glow.[34]

Two fabulous stones are noted by pseudo-Aristotle, and one of these, the ''sleeping-stone,'' must have possessed marvellous soporific power. It was a luminous stone of a bright ruddy hue, and shone in the darkness with a bright light. If a small quantity of this stone were

---

[32] ''Lithica,'' line 270.

[33] De Mely, '' La traité des fleuves de Plutarche,'' in Revue des Études Grecques, vol. v (1892), p. 331.

[34] Luciani, '' De Syria dea,'' cap. 32.

hung about a person's neck, he would sleep uninterrupt-
edly for three days and nights, and, when awakened on
the fourth day, he would still be almost overcome by sleep.
The other stone, of a greenish hue, had the opposite
quality and induced prolonged wakefulness; so long as
it was worn, sleep was banished. Our author gravely
states that "some men who must watch at night suffer
greatly from lack of sleep." If, however, they wore the
"waking-stone," they suffered no inconvenience from
their enforced vigils.[35] Evidently this stone would be a
precious possession for night-watchmen, and a more
satisfactory guarantee for their employers than "time-
clocks" or other tests of wakefulness.

In his commentary on Marbodus, Alardus of Amsterdam relates the history of a wonderful luminous stone, a
"chrysolampis," which, with many other precious stones,
was set in a marvellous golden tablet dedicated to St.
Adelbert, apostle of the Frisians and patron of the town
of Egmund (d. 720–730), by Hildegard, wife of Theodoric,
Count of Holland. The gift was made to the Abbey of
Egmund, where the saint's body reposed. Alardus tells
us that the "chrysolampis" shone so brightly that when
the monks were called to the chapel in the night-time,
they could read the Hours without any other light. This
wonderful stone was stolen by one of the monks, whom
Alardus terms "the most rapacious creature who ever
went on two legs"; but, fearing to keep so valuable a gem
with him, he cast it into the sea and it was never recovered.[36]

---

[35] Rose, " Aristoteles de lapidibus und Arnoldus Saxo," Zeitschr.
für D. Alt., New Series, vol. vi, 1875, pp. 375, 376.

[36] The abbey to which Hildegard gave the tablet was probably that
built by Theodoric II and destroyed by the Reformers in 1572. The
first building was of wood and was erected by Theodoric I in 923 or
924; this was ravaged by the Frisians not many years later.

Strange tales were told of a luminous "carbuncle" on the shrine of St. Elizabeth (d. 1231) at Marburg. This stone was set above the statuette of the Virgin, and it was said to emit fiery rays at night. However, Creuzer informs us that it was only a very brilliant rock crystal of a yellowish-white hue. The shrine was an elaborate work of art in silver gilt, and was literally covered with precious stones to the number of 824, besides two large pearls and a great many smaller ones. All these gems were stripped from their settings when the shrine was taken from Marburg to Cassel in 1810.[37]

At the Dusseldorf Exhibition of 1891, the writer saw what was called "The Ring of St. Elizabeth," purporting to be set with her miraculously luminous ruby. The stone in the setting proved, however, to be a large almost flat carbuncle garnet of no great brilliancy, set in a narrow rim of gold.

After noting the reports of medieval travellers regarding the wonderful luminous rubies of the sovereigns of Pegu and repeating the tale that the night was illumined by their splendor, Cleandro Arnobio adds that it did not appear that any such rubies were to be found in his day. Nevertheless, he had heard from an ecclesiastic of a certain jewel that shone brightly at night. This stone, however, was not a ruby, but was of a pale citron hue, and hence Arnobio inclines to believe that it was either a topaz or a yellow diamond.[38] This probably refers to the Marburg "carbuncle."

The luminous "ruby" of the King of Ceylon is noted by Chau Ju-Kua,[39] a Chinese writer of about the middle

---

[37] Creuzer, "Antik geschnittene Steine vom Grabmahl der heiligen Elizabeth," Leipsic and Darmstadt, 1834, pp. 25, 26.

[38] Arnobio, "Il tesoro delle gioie," Venice, 1602, p. 34.

[39] See the English translation of his "Chu-fan-chï," by Friedrich Hirth and W. W. Rockhill, St. Petersburg, 1911, p. 72.

of the thirteenth century and hence a contemporary of the Arab Teifashi. He says: "The king holds in his hand a jewel five inches in diameter, which cannot be burned by fire, and which shines in the night like a torch." This gigantic luminous gem was also believed to possess the virtues of an elixir of youth, for we are told that the king rubbed his face with it daily and by this means would retain his youthful looks even should he live more than ninety years.

The glories of Emperor Manuel's (ca. 1120–1180) throne are celebrated by the Hebrew traveller Benjamin of Tudela, who visited Constantinople in 1161 A.D. This splendid throne was of gold studded with precious stones and, suspended from the canopy by gold chains, hung a magnificent golden crown set with jewels of incalculable value and so bright and sparkling that their glitter rendered needless any other illumination at night.[40]

When Henry II of France (1519–1559) made his solemn entry into the city of Boulogne, a stranger from India presented to the sovereign a luminous stone. It was rather soft, had a fiery brilliance, and could not be touched with impunity. According to De Thou, this story was vouched for by J. Pipin, who saw the stone himself and described it in a letter to Antoine Mizauld, a writer on occult themes, well known in his day.[41]

Although Garcias ab Orta did not believe in the tales current in his time regarding luminous rubies, he relates a story of such a stone told to him by a gem-dealer. This man stated that he had purchased a number of fine but

---

[40] "Die Reisebeschreibung des R. Benjamin von Tudela," ed. by L. Grünhut and Marcus N. Adler, Jerusalem, 1903, pt. ii, trans., p. 17.

[41] Beckmann, "History of Inventions," English trans., London, 1846, vol. ii, p. 433.

small rubies from Ceylon, and had spread them out over a table. When he gathered them up again, one of the stones remained hidden in a fold of the table-cloth. In the night he remarked something like a flame emanating from the table. Lighting a candle, he approached the table and found there the small ruby; when this was removed and the candle extinguished, the light was no longer visible. Garcias admits that the gem-dealers were fond of telling good stories, but he concludes with the dictum, ''we must trust in them nevertheless.'' [42]

Not only the ruby, but the emerald also had the reputation of being a luminous stone, for, besides the shining ''emerald'' pillar in the temple of Melkart at Tyre, Pliny records the tale of a marble lion, with eyes of gleaming emeralds, which was set over the tomb of ''a petty king called Hermias.'' This tomb was on the coast, and the flashing light from the emerald eyes frightened away the tunny-fish, to the great loss of the fishermen. [43] Whether the eyes of the magnificent chryselephantine statue of Athene by Phidias were supposed to be luminous we do not know, but they were incrusted with precious stones. [44]

The collection of works by the English alchemists, published by Elias Ashmole, contains the tale of a worthy parson who lived in a little town near London, and who wished to immortalize himself by building across the Thames a bridge which would always be lighted at night. After relating several expedients which suggested themselves to him, the poet continues:

---

[42] Garcias ab Orta, '' Aromatum historia '' (Lat. version by Clusius), Antverpiæ, 1579, lib. i, p. 174.

[43] Plinii, '' Naturalis historia,'' lib. xxxvii, cap. 17.

[44] Platonis, '' Hippias major,'' ed. Didot, vol. i, p. 745.

At the laste he thought to make the light,
For the Bridge to shine by nighte,
With *Carbuncle Stones,* to make men wonder,
With double reflexion above and under:
Then new thought troubled his Minde
Carbuncle Stones how he might finde;

And where to find wise men and trewe,
Which would for his interest pursue,
In seeking all the Worlde about,
Plenty of Carbuncles to find out;
For this he took so mickle thought,
That his satt flesh wasted nigh to naught.[45]

It is scarcely necessary to add that the poor parson never realized his dream, but the story shows how popular was the belief that carbuncles or rubies shone with their own light.

A luminous or phosphorescent stone, which has been named the Bologna stone, is the subject of a treatise published by the physician Mentzel in 1675.[46] The writer describes various experiments made to test the peculiar qualities of this mineral, which is partly a radiated or crystalline sulphate of barytes, and phosphoresces when calcined. It was sometimes called the "lunar stone" (*lapis lunaris*), because, like the moon, it gave out in the darkness the light it received from the sun. Mentzel also relates that the stone was first discovered, in 1604, by Vincenzio Casscioroli, an adept in alchemy, who believed that it would be a great aid in the transmutation of the baser metals into gold, on account of its solar quality. The place of its occurrence was Monte Paterno, near

---

[45] Norton's " Ordinall "; in Ashmole " Theatrum Chemicum Britannicum," London, 1652, p. 27.

[46] Christiani Mentzelli, " Lapis Bononensis," Bilefeldiæ, 1675.

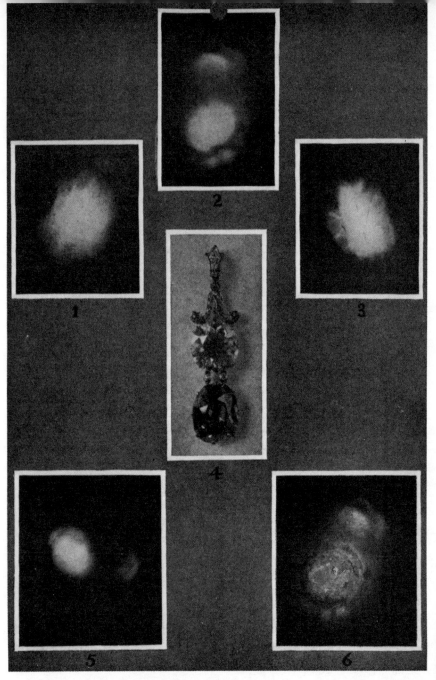

1. Self-print of upper diamond of No. 4 by phosphorescence, produced by rubbing briskly with stick covered by woolen cloth. Exposure one-half minute.

2. Self-print, both diamonds, after one minute's exposure to ultra-violet light, electric action eliminated.

3. Self-print, upper diamond. Exposure one-fourth minute.

4. Upper: blue-white Tiffanyite diamond, 14.86 carats; Bagagem Mine, Brazil. Lower: purple-black diamond, 13.35 carats; Brazil.

5. Self-print, both diamonds; different position.

6. Aspect of both diamonds (No. 4), one minute's exposure, ultra-violet light; blue-white phosphorescing white, purple-black having red glow.

Bologna, where it appeared in the fissures of the mountain, after torrential rains.

The various phenomena of fluorescence and phosphorescence undoubtedly explain some at least of the legends

SPECIMEN

DE

GEMMARVM

ORIGINE & VIRTVTIBVS.

IN QVO

Proponuntur & hiftoricè illuftantur quædam Conjeæuræ circa confiftentiam materiæ *Lapidum Pretioforum*, & fubjeæa, in quibus eorum præcipuæ virtutes confiftunt.

Ab Honoratiſſimo

ROBERTO BOYLE

NOBILI ANGLO, è SOCIETATE REGIA,

COLONIÆ ALLOBROGVM, Apud SAMVELEM DE TOVRNES.

M. DC. LXXX.

TITLE PAGE OF ROBERT BOYLE'S WORK ON THE ORIGIN AND VIRTUES OF GEMS.
Printed in Cologne in 1680.

regarding luminous stones, superstition or fantasy having here as in most other cases a certain substratum of fact. This class of physical phenomena has been made the subject of special investigation by the author, as many as 13,000 specimens of various minerals having been subjected to the most searching tests in order to determine their qualities in this respect.[47]   His interest in this field of research was greatly stimulated by a fortuitous happening.   In 1891 his wife, while hanging up a gown in a closet one evening, saw that the diamond in a ring she was wearing gave off a faint streak of light which was very noticeable in the dark, and this fact led to a long series of experiments on the fluorescence, phosphorescence, and triboluminescence of the diamond.[48] More than two centuries before, Robert Boyle made a similar set of experiments at night with a diamond which must have been an Indian stone, and which he describes as table cut, about one-third of an inch long and somewhat less in width; he remarks that it was a dull stone of very bad water, having a blemish with a whitish cloud covering nearly a third of the stone.[49]

The "Journal des Sçavans" for 1739 gives certain tests of the luminous quality of diamonds made by Mons. Du Fay.   In order successfully to observe this phenomenon, he prescribes that the experimenter shall remain in a darkened room for fifteen minutes, taking the additional precaution of closing one or both of his eyes.   The diamond to be tested should be exposed to the sun's rays, or to strong daylight, for less than a minute, and when taken into darkness the luminosity, if observable, lasts twelve

---

[47] See Kunz, " The Phosphorescence of the Diamond," Trans. N. Y. Academy of Sciences, vol. x, p. 50, 1890–91; Kunz and Baskerville, "The Action of Radium, Actinium, Roentgen rays, and Ultra Violet Light in Minerals and Gems," Science, vol. xviii, No. 468, pp. 769–783, December 18, 1903.

[48] See page 172.

[49] Boyle, " Works," London, 1744, vol. ii, p. 85.   The experiments were made October 27, 1663, and the results were communicated to the Royal Society the next day, the diamond which had been used being shown to the members at that time.

or thirteen minutes at longest. Not all diamonds show this quality, and nothing in their form or appearance serves to determine their possession of it. However, Mons. du Fay observed that the yellow diamonds, of which he tried a considerable number, were luminous. A single emerald, out of twenty that were tested, proved to be luminous.[50]

Boyle's experiments led to the discovery that some diamonds, when rubbed against wood or other hard substances, and even against cloth or silk, will emit a ray of light which seems to follow them; this is what is called triboluminescence.

The power of absorbing sunlight or artificial light and then giving it off in the dark is only possessed by certain diamonds. These are Brazilian stones, slightly milky in tint, or blue-white as they are often termed, and it is an included substance and not the diamond itself that possesses the power of storing up light and then giving it out. Willemite, kunzite, sphalerite (sulphide of zinc) and some other minerals possess the same power. Their peculiar property may be due to the presence of a slight quantity of manganese or to that of some of the uranium salts. That it is only the ultra-violet rays that are thus absorbed by these diamonds is proved by the fact that the phenomenon is not observable when a thin plate of glass is interposed between the sunlight or artificial light and the diamond, as glass is not traversed by these rays. The still undetermined substance to whose presence in diamonds of this type the special class of phenomena must be due, was named by the author

---

[50] " Journal des Sçavans," 1739, pp. 438, 439, of Amsterdam edition, citing " Hist. de l'Acad. Roy. des Sciences," 1735 (vol. xxxviii).

tiffanyite, in honor of the late Charles L. Tiffany (1812–1902), founder of the firm of Tiffany & Company.[51]

On the other hand all diamonds phosphoresce when exposed to the rays of radium, polonium, or actinium, even when glass is interposed. Treating of some of the aspects of phosphorescence in diamonds, Sir William Crookes says:[52]

In a vacuum, exposed to a high-tension current of electricity, diamonds phosphoresce of different colours, most South African diamonds shining with a bluish light. Diamonds from other localities emit bright blue, apricot, pale blue, red, yellowish-green, orange, and pale green light. The most phosphorescent diamonds are those which are fluorescent in the sun. One beautiful green diamond in my collection, when phosphorescing in a good vacuum, gives almost as much light as a candle, and you can easily read by its rays. But the time has hardly come when diamonds can be used as domestic illuminants!

By permission of Mrs. Kunz, wife of the well-known New York mineralogist, I will show you perhaps the most remarkable of all phosphorescing diamonds. This prodigy diamond will phosphoresce in the dark for some minutes after being exposed to a small pocket electric light, and if rubbed on a piece of cloth a long streak of phosphorescence appears.

The luminescence produced by heat is wonderfully marked in the case of chlorophane, a variety of fluorite. A Siberian specimen of a pale violet color emitted a white light merely from the heat of the hand; boiling water caused it to give out a green light, which was so greatly intensified when the specimen rested on a live coal that the radiance could be discerned from a considerable distance. Similar phenomena were observable in the case

---

[51] See Transactions of the New York Academy of Sciences, vol. xiv, p. 260; 1895.

[52] "Diamonds," a lecture delivered before the British Association at Kimberley, Sept. 5, 1905; London, 1905, p. 37. See also the same author's "Diamonds," London and New York, 1909, pp. 96–101.

ROCK-CRYSTAL BALL PENETRATED BY CRYSTALS OF RUTILE. MADAGASCAR.

of chlorophane from Amelia Court House, Va., and the writer found that specimens from this source also exhibited strong triboluminescence, resulting either from contact with one another, or with any hard substance.[53]

As the terms fluorescence and phosphorescence are sometimes rather carelessly employed, it may be well to note here that while both terms are used to denote the luminescence of a non-luminous body resulting from the action of light rays, of the electric current, or of radiant energy of any kind, as well as from heat, fluorescence signifies a luminosity which only continues so long as the exciting cause is present, while phosphorescence means a luminosity persisting for a longer or shorter period after the exciting cause has ceased to operate directly. The latter term therefore denotes a luminous energy stored up in the formerly non-luminous body and emitted by it for a certain time, at the expiration of which it again becomes non-luminous. Other special designations of induced luminosity in minerals are triboluminescence, the emission of light as a result of friction and thermoluminescence, a term used to denote light-emission excited by moderate heating, even by the warmth of the hand.

An old treatise in Greek, said in its title to come from "the sanctuary of the temple," and containing material, partly of Egyptian origin, may help us to understand something of the processes employed by a temple priest to impress the common people by the sight of luminous gems. The writer of the treatise declares that for the production of "the carbuncle that shines in the night" use was made of certain parts (he says "the

[53] Kunz, "Gems and Precious Stones of North America," New York, 1890, pp. 183, 184.

bile") of marine animals whose entrails, scales and bones exhibited the phenomenon of phosphorescence. If properly treated, precious stones (preferably carbuncles) would glow so brightly at night "that anyone owning such a stone could read or write by its light as well as he could by daylight.[54]

In the *Annales de Chimie et Physique,* the great French chemist, M. Berthelot, discusses this matter and expresses the following opinion: [55]

" The texts leave no room for doubt as to the employment by the ancients of precious stones rendered phosphorescent in the dark by the superficial application of tinctures composed of materials whose phosphorescent quality is known to us. Although this luminescence, due to an application of organic oxidizable materials, could not well be durable, still it might be made to last several hours, perhaps several days, and it could always be renewed by repeating the application."

The use of jewelled ornaments to heighten by their luminosity in obscurity or in darkness the effect produced by a sacred image, and to stimulate religious awe in the beholder, is testified to by the ultra-Protestant traveller, Fynes Moryson, Gent., who went to Italy in 1594. Of his visit to the Santa Casa in Loreto, he says that he himself and two Dutchmen, his companions, were permitted to enter the inner chapel of the sanctuary, "where," he proceeds, "we did see the Virgin's picture, adorned with pretious Jewels, and the place (to increase religious horror) being darke, yet the Jewels shined by the light of wax candles." Although there is no question here of naturally luminous gems, this might have

---

[54] " Collection des anciens alchemistes grecs," ed. by M. Berthelot, trans., p. 336–338; text pp. 351, 352, Paris, 1887, 1888.

[55] " Sur un procédé antique pour rendre les pierres précieuses et les vitrifications phosphorescentes," Annales de Chimie et Physique, 6th ser., vol. xiv, pp. 429–432.

been the impression produced upon a more sympathetic pilgrim.[56]

Writing of the traditions in regard to luminous stones, Sir Richard F. Burton says, "There may be a basis of fact to this fancy, the abnormal effect of precious stones upon mesmeric sensitives."[57]   However, while some instances are recorded of psychic impression produced by precious stones on the minds of persons possessing a highly sensitive nervous system, it seems likely that some legends of luminous stones had their origin in the refractive powers of cut gems, by means of which a dim and distant light would be reflected from the surface of the stones and would seem to spring from them. Quite possibly, in other instances, there was a disposition to cater to the popular belief by placing a light so that the hidden beams traversed the stone and appeared to emanate from it.

---

[56] Moryson, "An Itinerary containing his Ten Yeeres Travell through the Twelve Dominions," etc., Glasgow, 1907–8, vol. i. p. 216.

[57] Burton, "Supplementary Nights," London, 1886, vol. iii, p. 354, note.

VI

On Crystal Balls and Crystal Gazing

WE have evidence of the use of crystal balls as means of divination in medieval times, and "scrying" in some of its many forms was by no means rare in the Greek and Roman periods. The essential requisite for the exercise of this species of divination is a polished surface of some sort upon which the scryer shall gaze intently; for this purpose mirrors, globules of lead or quicksilver, polished steel, the surface of water, and even pools of ink, have been employed and have been found to insure quite as satisfactory results as the crystal ball. The points of light reflected from the polished surface (*points de repère*) serve to attract the attention of the gazer and to fix the eye until, gradually, the optic nerve becomes so fatigued that it finally ceases to transmit to the sensorium the impression made from without and begins to respond to the reflex action proceeding from the brain of the gazer. In this way the impression received from within is apparently projected and seems to come from without. It is easy to understand that the results must vary according to the idiosyncrasy of the various scryers; for everything depends upon the sensitiveness of the optic nerve. In many cases the effect of prolonged gazing upon the brilliant surface will simply produce a loss of sight, the optic nerve will be temporarily paralyzed and will as little respond to stimulation from within as from without; in other cases, however, the nerve will be only deadened as regards external impressions, while retaining sufficient activity to react against a stimulus

191

from the brain centres. It is almost invariably stated that, prior to the appearance of the desired visions, the crystal seems to disappear and a mist rises before the gazer's eye.

The Achaians, as Pausanius relates, frequently used a mirror to divine diseases or to learn whether there was danger of sudden death. Of the Temple of Demeter, or Ceres, at Patras, he writes: [1]

In front of the temple of Demeter there is a well. A stone wall separates this well from the temple, but steps lead down to it from the outside. Here there is an infallible oracle, although it does not answer all questions, but only those touching diseases. They attach a slender cord to a mirror and let it down into the well, balancing it carefully so that the water does not cover the face, but only touches the rim. Then, after making a prayer to the goddess and burning incense to her, they look into the mirror, and it shows whether the sick person will die or recover. Such is the power of truth in this water.

This sacred well with its oracle of the magic mirror must have been in Lucian's mind when, in his description of the palace of the Moon-King, he says: [2]

Another wonderful thing I saw in the palace. Suspended over a rather shallow well there is a large mirror, and anyone who goes down into this well will hear every word that is spoken on earth, while, if he gazes on the mirror, he will see there every city and every nation just as clearly as though he were looking down upon them from a slight elevation. At the time I was there, I saw my native country and its inhabitants. Whether I myself was seen by them in turn, I am not sure.

Lucian adds, with a fine touch of irony, "Anyone who doubts this assertion needs only to go there himself and he will find out that I speak the truth." As no one has

---

[1] Pausaniæ, "Descriptio Græciæ," ed. Schubart, vol. ii, Lipsiæ, 1883, pp. 54, 55, lib. ii, cap, 21, 12.

[2] Luciani, " Vera Historia," lib. i, 26.

yet made a trip to the moon, the assertion is still uncontradicted.

In their religious legends the ancient Mexicans taught that their god Tezcatlipuco had a magic mirror in which he saw everything that happened in the world.[3] He was sometimes named Necocyautl, "sower of discord," because he often stirred up war and strife among men, but he was also lord of riches and prosperity, which he bestowed and took away again at his will. To the influence of this divinity were attributed many omens and certain strange visions, announced by repeated knockings.[4]

In the Orphic poem "Lithica," a magic sphere of stone is described. The substance is called "sideritis" or "ophitis," and is said to be black, round, and heavy; possibly some metal, rather than a stone, is designated by these names. Helenus, the Trojan soothsayer, is said to have used this sphere to foretell the downfall of his native city. He fasted for twenty-one days and then wrapped the sphere in soft garments, like an infant, and offered sacrifices to it until, by the magic of his prayers, "a living soul warmed the precious substance."

A strange variety of divination by means of mirrors placed on the heads of boys, who, with eyes blindfolded, were supposed to perceive forms or signs of some description in the mirrors, is noted by Spartianus in his life of the Emperor Didius Julianus (ca. 133–193). This ruler is said to have resorted to this form of divination, and the boy entrusted with the task is asserted to have

---

[3] Balz, "Die sogenannte magische Spiegel und ihr Gebrauch"; Archiv für Anthrop. N.S., vol. ii, p. 45, 1904.

[4] Sahagun, "Historia general de las cosas de Nueva España," Mexico, 1829, vol. i, pp. 2, 3; vol. ii, pp. 6, 12, 16, 17; lib. i, cap. 3; lib. v, cap. 3, 9, 11, 12.

announced the approaching accession of Septimius Severus (146–211) and the dethronement of Didius Julianus.[5]

An indication that the usage of divination by means of a silver cup existed among the primitive Hebrews has been found in the story of Joseph and his brethren. In Genesis xliv, 1–5, we read that Joseph concealed a silver cup in the sack of grain borne away by Benjamin, making of this a pretext for requiring the return of his brethren. He sent messengers to overtake them and directed them to demand the return of the cup, using these words: "Is not this it in which my lord drinketh, and whereby indeed he divineth?"

The Arabic author, Haly Abou Gefar, tells of a golden ball used by "the Magi, followers of Zoroaster," in their incantations. It was incrusted with celestial symbols and set with a sapphire, and one of these magicians, after attaching it to a strip of bullhide, swung it around, reciting at the same time various spells and incantations.[6] Probably the magician, by fixing his gaze upon the brilliant revolving sphere, gradually fell into a hypnotic trance, during which visions appeared to him. These he could afterward interpret to those who had sought his aid to read the future, or obtain information regarding things that were happening far away.

An important side-light on the beliefs of Western Europe, in the fifth century, regarding crystal-gazing, is afforded by one of the canons of the synod held about 450 A.D. by St. Patrick and the bishops Auxilius and Issernanus. Here it is decreed that any Christian who believes there is a Lamia (or witch) in the mirror is to be anathe-

---

[5] Spartiani, "Vita Didii Juliani," cap 7.

[6] Reichelti, "De amuletis," Argentorati, 1676, p. 36.

matized, and is not to be again received into the Church unless he shall have renounced this belief and shall have diligently performed the penance imposed upon him.[7] In this case, as in many others, the vision in the crystal or mirror did not represent some former or contemporaneous happening, but the figure of an evil spirit, who, either by signs or words, imparted to the scryer the information he was seeking.

The power to see images of evil spirits on the surface of water was claimed by those called *hydromantii* in the ninth century. This is attested in a work composed about 860 A.D. by Hincmar, Archbishop of Rheims, who characterizes the supposed appearances as "images or deceptions of the demons." These diviners asserted that they received audible communications from the spirits, and they therefore evidently believed that the appearances were realities.[8]

Although, as we have seen, many different materials were used for scrying, the preference was often given to polished spheres of beryl; in modern times, however, the rock-crystal is considered the best adapted for the purpose.

In his introduction to "Crystal Gazing," by N. W. Thomas,[9] Andrew Lang writes of what he terms hypnagogic illusions—images which appear when the eyes are closed and before sleep supervenes. When faces appeared to him in this way, they were always unfamiliar ones, with the single exception of having once seen his own face in profile. The same was almost invariably true

---

[7] "Synodum episcorporum Patricii, Auxilii et Issernani," in Migne, Patr. Lat., vol. liii, Parisiis, 1865, col. 825.

[8] Hincmari, "Opera Omnia," in Migne, Patr. Lat., vol. cxxv, col. 7; De devortio Lotharii et Tetbergæ.

[9] London, 1905, pp. xxiv, xxx.

GLASS BALL, PERFORATED AND MOUNTED IN METAL, SO THAT IT CAN BE SUSPENDED AND USED FOR OCCULT AND CURATIVE PURPOSES.

Period of about tenth or twelfth century. Collection of Sir Charles Hercules Read.

BALL OF JET, PERFORATED, MOUNTED IN METAL, SO THAT IT CAN BE SUSPENDED AND USED FOR OCCULT AND CURATIVE PURPOSES.

Period of about tenth or twelfth century. Collection of Sir Charles Hercules Read.

EYE AGATE, SHOWING A NUMBER OF CIRCULAR MARKINGS.

Mounted in metal and kept in a box, as a votive or curative stone. About fourteenth century. British Museum. (See page 149.)

of landscape and inanimate objects. These forms seemed to grow out of the bright points of light which frequently appear when the eyes are closed, and Lang suggests a similar origin for the visions of the "scryers"—namely, the development of the images from dark or light points in the glass.

In regard to this, we have an interesting passage in the works of Ibn Kaldoun, a Persian writer, born in 1332, who gives the following very acute analysis of the phenomena accompanying crystal-gazing.[10]

Some believe that the image perceived in this way takes form on the surface of the mirror, but they are mistaken. The diviner looks at this surface fixedly until it disappears, and a curtain, like a mist, is interposed between him and the mirror. Upon this curtain are designed the forms he wishes to see, and this permits him to give indications, either affirmative or negative, concerning the matter on which he is questioned. He then describes his perceptions as he has received them. The diviners, while in this state, do not see what is really to be seen (in the mirror); it is another kind of perception, which is born in them and which is realized not by sight but by the soul.

As to the character and quality of the crystal to be used, Abbot Tritheim, the master of the famous Cornelius Agrippa, says:[11]

Procure of a lapidary a good, clear, pellucid crystal of the bigness of a small orange,—i.e., about one inch and a half in diameter; let it be globular, or round each way alike; then you have got this crystal fair and clear, without any clouds or specks. Get a small plate of pure gold to encompass the crystal round one-half; let this be fitted on an ivory or ebony pedestal. Let there be engraved a circle round the crystal; afterwards the name: Tetragrammaton. On the other side of the plate let there be engraved, Michael, Gabriel, Uriel, Raphael, which are the four principal angels ruling over the Sun, Moon, Venus, and Mercury.

---

[10] Ibn Kaldoun, in Notices et Ext. de MSS. de la Bib. Imp., vol. xix, p. 221.

[11] See Barrett, " The Magus," London, 1801, p. 135.

The four letters constituting the Tetragrammaton are
the Hebrew characters *yôdh, hê, wâw* and *hê,* יהוה. As
this divine name was regarded in later Judaism as too
sacred to be pronounced, the word lord, *adonai,* was substituted for it in the reading of the Scriptures. For
this reason, when the vowel signs were added to the text
to indicate the traditional pronunciation, the consonants
Yhwh were provided with the vowels of *adonai* and the
name was therefore read Jehovah by Christian scholars.

The Persian poet Jâmi writes thus of a magic mirror
in the poem "Salamân and Absal": [12]

> Then from his secret Art the Sage Vizyr
> A Magic Mirror made; a Mirror like
> The bosom of All-wise Intelligence,
> Reflecting in its mystic compass all
> Within the sev'nfold volume of the World
> Invol'd; and looking in that Mirror's face
> The Shah beheld the face of his Desire.

Roger Bacon (1214–1292) was probably the most
gifted man of the thirteenth century, and his writings
testify to an extraordinarily clear perception of the essential principles of scientific research. However, his true
greatness was not generally appreciated in his own age,
and popular fancy wove about his name a fabric of
legend in which he appeared as an arch-necromancer and
magician. The curious old work entitled "The Famous
Historie of Fryar Bacon" gives a number of the strange
recitals which became current in England in regard to
Bacon's wonderful powers.

One of these treats of a marvellous "glass" made by
the friar, in which events happening at far-distant places

---

[12] Jâmi's "Salamân and Absal," trans. by Edward Fitzgerald, Boston, 1899, p. 84.

were mirrored. On one occasion two young men, between whom the friendliest feelings existed, came to
Bacon and requested him to let them see in the mirror
what their fathers were doing at the time. The friar con-
sented, but the experiment, while successful, was the
cause of a terrible misfortune. The story is as follows:

The Fathers of these two Gentlemen (in their Sonnes absence)
were become great foes: this hatred betweene them was growne to that
height, that wheresoever they met, they had not onely wordes, but
blowes. Just at that time, as it should seeme, that their Sonnes were
looking to see how they were in health, they were met, and had drawne,
and were together by the eares. Their Sonnes seeing this, and having
been alwayes great friends, knew not what to say to one another, but
beheld each other with angry lookes. At last one of their Fathers,
as they might perceive in the Glasse, had a fall, and the other, taking
advantage, stood over him ready to strike him. The Sonne of him
that was downe could then containe himselfe no longer, but told the
other young man, that his Father had received wrong. He answered
againe, that it was faire. At last there grew such foule words betweene
them, and their bloods were so heated, that they presently stabbed the
one the other with their Daggers, and so fell downe dead.

The sceptre of the Scottish regalia is surmounted by
a crystal globe, two inches and a quarter in diameter,
and the mace by a large crystal beryl. In former times
these stones were regarded as amulets and their use was
traced back to the Druids. Sir Walter Scott tells us that
in his time they were still known among the Scottish
Highlanders as "Stones of Power." [13]
The testimony of John of Salisbury (1120?–1180)
shows that in the twelfth century, in England, divination
by means of the arts of the *specularii* was often practised. The prelate writes that when a boy, he himself and
a companion a few years older received instruction from

---

[13] Description of the Regalia of Scotland, by Sir Walter Scott,
Bart., Edinburg, n. d., p. 13.

a priest who was addicted to the use of these magic arts. This priest used to polish the finger-nails of the boys with a consecrated oil or ointment, and then direct them to look upon the polished surface until some figure or form should appear. Sometimes the smooth, polished surface of a basin was used. John of Salisbury regarded it as a mark of divine favor that he himself saw nothing upon the smooth and lustrous surface, but he states that his companion observed certain vague and shadowy forms. Certain names pronounced by the priest on these occasions terrified the boy, for he believed them to be the names of evil spirits; indeed, such was his reluctance to participate in the unholy rites that his presence was believed to interfere with the production of the phenomena.[14]

In another part of his "Policraticus," John of Salisbury states that the specularii claimed that their gift of seeing visions on polished surfaces was never used to injure any one, but was often useful in the detection of theft and in counteracting magic spells.[15]

Under the comprehensive chapter heading: "How to conjure the crystal so that all things may be seen in it," Paracelsus (1493–1541) declares that "to conjure" means nothing more than "to observe anything rightly, to learn and to understand what it is." The crystal was of the nature of the air, and hence all things movable and immovable that could be seen in the air could also be seen in the crystal or *speculum*.[16]

---

[14] Johannis Saresberensis, "Policraticus," Lyon, 1513, fols. lxxvii, verso, lxxviii, recto, lib. ii, cap. 28.

[15] Johannis Saresberensis, l. c., fol. lxxvi, recto, lib. ii, cap. 28.

[16] "The Hermetic and Alchemical writings of Aureolus Philippus Theophrastus Bombast of Hohenheim, called Paracelsus the Great," trans. by Arthur Edward Waite, London, 1894, vol. i, p. 224.

Paracelsus showed keen insight, and his conclusions are excellent. One might add, however, that it is a fact that these are images condensed in the double convex lens, forming as it were, an internal crystal sphere. These images are reversed, distorted and twisted, and when they become visible to one who is expecting strange things, they form mental impressions which it is often very difficult to erase. Many crystal gazers are frequently very highly wrought, nervous and susceptible, and other influences uniting with the impressions produced, may give the brain for a time the power to evolve kaleidoscopic effects.

Directions for the use of an Erdenspiegel, or "earth-mirror," are given in an old German manuscript written in 1658 by a Capuchin priest.[17] The mirror is to be set about two inches above a board, and the questions to be answered are to be placed beneath it. The scryer is recommended to place three grains of salt upon his tongue, whereupon he is to repeat a prayer and cross himself. He now takes the mirror in his hand and breathes upon it three times, repeating the words, "In the name of the Father, of the Son, and of the Holy Spirit. Amen."

These preliminaries having been accomplished, the following prayer, or rather invocation, is repeated:

O thou holy Archangel N. N., I pray to thee most fervently through the great and unsearchable name of the Lord of all Lords and King of all Kings, Jod, He, Vau, He, Tetragrammaton, Adonay, Schaday, receive my greeting and give ear to the humble petition which I offer in the name of the great and highest God, Elohim, Zebaoth, that thou shalt appear to me in the world-mirror, and give me knowledge and instruction in answer to my questions.

---

[17] "Unterricht vom Gebrauch des Erdspiegels, 1658" (Aus dem Kapuziner-Kloster in Immenstat. Eine Handschrift des Kapuziner-Paters Franziscus Seraph. Heider daselbst); in "Handschriftlichen Schätze aus Kloster Bibliotheken," Köln am Rhein, 1734–1810 (reprint).

The strong religious tone of these directions for the use of the mirror and the fact that it is a priest who gives them, shows that there was a disposition to tolerate the employment of such "white magic."

In medieval times it was believed that the vision in the crystal was produced through the agency of an indwelling spirit, and, therefore, it was necessary to use some very potent spell to force this spirit to enter the stone. Many of these ancient spells have been preserved, and they contain a strange and incongruous mixture of religious and magical formulas. In one of these, dating from the end of the fifteenth century, after a recitation of a long and rambling conjuration, we read, "And y^{en} ask ye chylde yf h^e seethe any thyng, and yf no, let the m^r begin his conjuratyō agayn." As usual the scrying was done by a child, the conjuration being spoken by the minister. An important part of the conjuration consisted in the repetition of a number of divine names, most of them originally Hebrew, but so much corrupted by reciters who did not know their meaning that it is now exceedingly difficult to interpret them correctly.

A proof that this form of magic was often regarded as quite compatible with religion is offered us in a passage from a sixteenth century manuscript,[18] where we read that the crystal should be laid on the altar "on the Side that the gospell is read on. And let the priest say a mass on the same Side." If the conjuration is successful, the same manuscript tells us that "these angells being once appeared will not depart the glasse or stone untill the Sonne be sett except you licence them." It also seems that "scrying" was looked upon as a special gift, only granted to a favored few as a peculiar privilege, and we

---

[18] Sloane MS. 3851, f. 50b.

read that "Prayer and a good beleefe prevailed much. For faith is the cay to this and all other works, and without it nothing can be effected." The child scryer, either maid or boy, should not be more than twelve years old.

That a certain religious spirit, however mistaken, often animated the crystal-gazers of the sixteenth century, is shown in the case of the "speculator" of John a Windor, who confessed that when he led an impure life the "dæmons" would not appear to him in his glass. He would then proceed to fumigate the apartment, as though believing that the very air was contaminated by the sins of the operator. We may hope that the seer was not content with this, but also tried to reform his evil ways. Another scryer, a woman named Sarah Skelhorn, declared that the spirits that appeared to her in the glass would often follow her about the house from room to room, so that she at last became weary of their presence.[19] Both of these scryers had regular employment, for it was quite customary for a gentleman to have a household seer, just as he would have a body-physician, if he could afford it.

A sixteenth century work on magic, the "Höllenzwang" of Dr. Faustus, whose name has been immortalized for all ages by Goethe, gives very particular and detailed directions for the preparation and consecration of a crystal, whether glass or quartz. Faust asks his "Mephistophelis" whether such crystals can be made, and the spirit replies: "Yes, indeed, my Faust," and directs Faust to go, on a Tuesday, to a glass-maker, and get the latter to form a glass. It was requisite that this

---

[19] Jonson, "The Alchemist," ed. Hathaway, New York, 1903, pp. 101, 145, note.

work should be done in the hour of Mars, that is, in the first, eighth, fifteenth or twenty-second hour of Tuesday. The crystal when completed must not be accepted as a gift, but a price must be paid for it. When the object had been secured, Mephistopheles directs that it be buried in a grave, where it must be left for the space of three weeks; it was then to be unearthed; if a woman purchased it, she must bury it in a woman's grave. However, these preliminaries only served to prepare the crystal for the final consecration, as the mere material mass was regarded as inert and possessing no virtue until certain spirits were summoned to dwell within it. Mephistopheles confesses that he alone would not be powerful enough, and he directs Faust to call upon the spirits Azeruel and Adadiel also. Faust is assured that the three spirits will show him in the crystal whatever he may wish to know. If anything has been stolen, the thief will appear; if any one is suffering from disease, the character of his malady will be revealed, etc.[20]

Another way of preparing a crystal glass or mirror is given in the same work. After the glass has been bought it is to be immersed in baptismal water in which a first-born male child has been baptized, and therein it is to remain for three weeks. The water is then to be poured out over a grave and the sixth chapter of the Revelation of St. John is to be read. Hereupon the following conjuration should be pronounced:

O crystal, thou art a pure and tender virgin, thou standest at one of the gates of heaven, that nothing may be hidden from thee; thou standest under a cloud of heaven that nothing may be hidden from

---

[20] Keisewetter, "Faust in der Geschichte und Tradition," Leipzig, 1893, p. 472.

DR. DEE'S SHEW STONE.

Natural size. British Museum. This sphere of smoky-quartz came to the British Museum in 1700 with the Cottonian Library, donated at that time by the grandson of the original collector, Sir Robert Bruce Cotton (1571-1631).

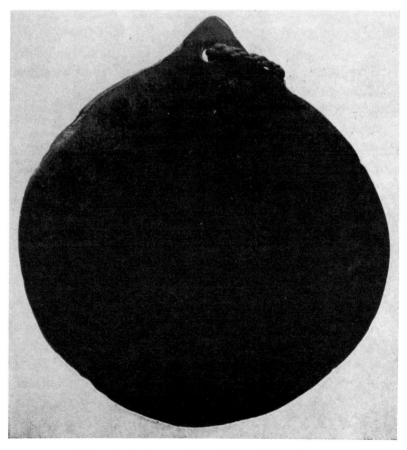

OBSIDIAN MIRROR, WITH NATIVE TEXTILE STRING.

Used by Aztecs and ancient Mexicans for various purposes. British Museum. Identical in shape and size with that known as "Dr. Dee's Mirror," now in the possession of Prince Alexis Soltykoff, of Russia. This was enclosed in a leather-covered case.

thee, whether in fields or meadows, whether master or servant, whether wife or maid. Let this be said to thee in the name of God, as a plea for thy help.[21]

The visions seen in crystal gazing were often supposed to be the work of evil spirits, seeking to seduce the souls of men by offering the promise of riches or by according them an unlawful glimpse into the future. Here, as in other magical operations, there was both white and black magic, recourse being had in some cases to good, and in others to evil spirits. As an illustration of the latter practice, a sixteenth century writer relates that in the city of Nuremberg, some time during the year 1530, a "demon" showed to a priest, in a crystal, the vision of a buried treasure. Believing in the truth of this vision, the priest went to the spot indicated, where he found an excavation in the form of a cavern, in the depths of which he could see a chest and a black dog lying alongside it. Eagerly the priest entered the cavern, hoping to possess himself of the treasure, but the top of the excavation caved in and he was crushed to death.[22]

The famous charlatan, Dr. Dee, who was for a time a prominent figure at the court of Emperor Rudolph II, was highly favored by Queen Elizabeth. The queen visited him several times, and even appears to have consulted him on political matters. In his diary the doctor relates that the queen called at his house shortly after his wife's death, which took place March 16, 1575. Of this visit he gives the following details:

The Queen's Majestie, with her most honorable Privy Council, and other the Lords and Nobility, came purposely to have visited my library: but finding that my wife was within four hours before buried

---

[21] Keisewetter, " Faust in der Geschichte und Tradition, p. 473.
[22] Wieri, " De prestigiis demonum," Basileæ, 1563, p. 121.

out of the house, her Majestie refused to come in; but willed to fetch my glass so famous, and to show unto her some of the properties of it, which I did. Her Majestie being taken down from her horse by the Earle of Liecester, Master of the Horse, at the church wall of Mortlake, did see some of the properties of that glass, to her Majestie's great contentment and delight.[23]

It was at Mortlake, on December 22, 1581, that Dr. Dee made his first essay with his crystal ball. The proceedings were conducted with a certain religious ceremonial, and began with a pious invocation to the angel of the stone. This celestial being soon graciously deigned to manifest himself in the stone and—presumably by the voice of the scryer—answered the questions put by those present.

There can be little doubt that Dee used more than one crystal in the course of his experiments; that now in the British Museum is of cairngorm, or "smoky-quartz." This variety of quartz may have been chosen because of the Scotch superstitions regarding its virtues; for, as a rule, charlatans seek to avail themselves of already existing superstitions in order to make their innovations more acceptable.

To give assurance to those who consulted such crystals that no diabolical agency was involved in the production of the phenomena, it was customary that a child should be the crystal-gazer. In Dr. Dee's experiments, however, it was usually the notorious Kelley, his *âme damnée,* who undertook this task of interpreting the crystal visions. The description given by Dee of a little girl who frequently acted as the intermediary of the higher powers suggests one of the fanciful

[23] " The Private Diary of Dr. John Dee," ed. by Halliwell, London, 1842 (Camden Soc. Pub.), p. 9, note (" Compendious Memorial," p. 516).

creations of our great novelist Hawthorne. Her mystic name was Madimi, and she is depicted as a pretty girl about eight years old, and with long flowing hair. To make her appearance more conspicuous, she was attired in a silk dress with chatoyant effects in red and green. At times, during the séances, this gay little figure could be seen flitting about the study, rendered even more whimsical and strange from its contrast with the piles of dusty old books, the curiosities, and the magical instruments collected there.[24]

This visionary maiden Madimi, of whom Dee relates so much in his diary, was apparently a child of fancy, a creation of Kelley's fertile brain. The diary is somewhat obscure in this particular and easily misunderstood; but there can be little doubt that where Madimi is represented as speaking, it is Kelley's voice that transmits to Dee her revelations. One passage, often overlooked, gives evidence of this. Madimi has appeared and is addressing her remarks to Kelley and to Dee by turns; finally, Dee says, "I know you see me often and I see you only by faith and imagination." To this Madimi quickly retorts, "pointing to E. K." (Kelley), "That sight is perfecter than his." Evidently we must understand this to signify something that Kelley has told Dee, for the latter's words show that he did not himself see the little fairy pointing to his friend. In many respects little Madimi may recall another "spiritual" maiden of whom we heard much a few years ago, the sprightly little Indian spirit "Bright Eyes," whose love for candy and jewelry was so very earthly.

---

[24] A true and faithful Relation of what passed for Many Yeeres between Dr. John Dee and Some Spirits. With preface by Meric. Casaubon, London, 1659, p. 1.

Not only the quality of the crystal had to be considered, but also its support and surroundings. Of this we have an interesting instance in the case of Dr. Dee's crystal. In one of his manuscripts is recorded the fact that on the 10th of March, 1582, Kelley saw in the crystal a representation of the form and arrangement of the table on which it should be set; particular instructions on the matter were also directly imparted to the scryer by the angel Uriel. The table was to be square, measuring two cubits each way and two cubits in height; and it was to have four feet. The material was to be "swete wood" and upon it was to be placed the Sigillum Dei (Seal of God) impressed upon the purest, colorless wax, the disk being 1⅛ inches thick and 9 inches in diameter. It bore a cross and the magic letters A. G. L. A., a transliteration into Roman characters of the initials of the Hebrew words signifying "Thou are great forever, O Lord." Four other and smaller seals were to be provided, one to be placed under each leg of the table; each of these seals being impressd with geometrical figures within or upon which were the seven sacred names of God and the names of the seven angels ruling the seven planetary heavens; Zabothiel, Zedekiel, Madiniel, Semeliel [Semeshiel], Nogabiel, Corabiel [Cocabiel] and Levaniel, the angels, respectively, of Saturn, Jupiter, Mars, the Sun, Venus, Mercury and the Moon. There then appeared to the scryer the figure of the table with the crystal resting upon it. Of this it is said: [25]

"Under the table did seeme to be layd red sylk to lye four square somewhat broader than the table, hanging down with four knops or tassells at the four corners

[25] See B. M. Dalton's notes in the Proceedings of the Society of Antiquaries, 2d ser., vol. xxi, 380–383. Sloane MS. A. 3188.

thereof. Uppon the uppermost red silk did seme to be set the stone with the frame, right over and uppon the principal seal, saving that the sayd sylk was betwene the one and the other.''

It therefore seems that the prejudice in favor of a black or at least a dark background for the crystal did not appeal to Dr. Dee, and indeed the effect of color may perhaps better serve to neutralize troublesome reflections than does black.

The personages Kelley pretended to see in or around the magic crystal were described by him to Dr. Dee in the greatest detail, and this undoubtedly served to lend more reality and authority to their communications. As an illustration of Kelley's inventiveness in this matter, we may take his description of ''Nalvage,'' a spirit that first appeared while the doctor and his famulus were in Cracow, April 10, 1584, and was subsequently a frequent visitor. The seer introduces his new ''control'' as follows: [26]

He hath a Gown of white silk, with a Cape with three pendants with tassels on the end of them all green; it is fur, white, and seemeth to shine, with a wavering glittering. On his head is nothing, he hath no berd. His phisiognomy is like the pictures of King Edward the Sixth; his hair hangeth down a quarter of the length of the Cap, somewhat curling, yellow. He hath a rod or wand in his hand, almost as big as my little finger; it is of Gold, and divided into three equal parts, with a brighter Gold than the rest. He standeth upon his round table of Christal, or rather Mother of Pearl.

When reading the words spoken by Kelley and so carefully preserved by Dr. Dee, we are reminded, aside from the archaic turn of speech, of the minute descriptions so glibly given by modern mediums. It is true that

---

[26] Casaubon's '' Relation,'' p. 73.

lately, in America, the spirits of the former owners of
the land, of the blameless aborigines, seem to have acquired a quasi monopoly of the intercourse with the
other world.

Most of the early records of crystal-gazing show conclusively enough that the images revealed in the stone
were produced by the expectations, the hopes, or the
fears of the gazer. In many cases, indeed, the vision is
only prophetic because it determines the future conduct
of the person who consults the stone. Fully persuaded
that what has been seen must come to pass, he, or she,
proceeds more or less consciously to make it happen, to
fulfil the prediction.

As an instance of this we may take from an old German book [27] the tale of a lovelorn maiden who seeks the
aid of an enchantress to learn whether she will marry
her lover, upon whom her parents look with disfavor.
The mystic crystal is brought out wrapped in a yellow
handkerchief, and is placed in a green bowl beneath
which is spread a blue cloth, the reflections from these
different colors being probably calculated to stimulate
the optic nerve and favor the appearance of some picture upon the polished surface of the crystal. The young
girl, in rapt attention, looks long and earnestly; at last
she cries out that she sees her own form and that of her
lover. Both look pale and sad, and they appear to be
about to set forth upon a long and perilous journey, for
the lover wears riding-boots and carries a brace of pis-
tols. The girl is so terrified at the sight that she faints
away. The sequel of this vision is a runaway match, and
we can easily understand that when the lover proposed

---

[27] Rist, "Die Aller-Edelste Zeit-Verkürtung der ganzen Welt,"
Franckfurt on dem Mayn, 1668, p. 255.

this adventure, the girl believed that it was written in the book of fate and willingly agreed to undertake it.

The great humorous poem "Hudibras," wherein all the foibles of the seventeenth century are castigated, does not fail to make mention of Dee and Kelley and their crystal. Of the sorcerer whose aid Hudibras seeks we are told: [28]

> He'd read Dee's prefaces before,
> The Dev'l and Euclid o'er and o'er;
> And all th' intrigues 'twixt him and Kelley,
> Lascus and th' Emperor, would tell ye.
>
> Kelley did all his feats upon
> The devil's looking-glass, a stone
> Where, playing with him at bo-peep
> He solved all problems ne'er so deep.

In his experiments in crystal-gazing, Dr. Dee evidently used more than one crystal, and did not indeed confine the operations of his scryer or scryers to brilliant spheres. In the collection of Horace Walpole, at Strawberry Hill, was a polished slab of black stone, obsidian, from Mexico. This came into the possession of Mr. Smythe Piggott and later (1853) into that of Lord Londesborough; it is now in the collection of Prince Alexis Soltykoff. Horace Walpole wrote a label for the stone, in which he says that it had long been owned by the Mordaunts, Earls of Petersborough, and was described in the catalogue of their collection as the black stone into which Dr. Dee used to call his spirits. Later it was owned by John Campbell, Duke of Argyle, who gave it to Horace Wal-

---

[28] Butler, "Hudibras," Part II, Canto III, 11, 235–8, and 631–4. This second part was issued in 1663, four years after Casaubon's publication of Dee's journal.

pole.[29]   Undoubtedly any polished surface, whether flat
or convex, might serve the purpose of the scryer almost
equally well; the possible advantage of a convex or a
spherical form consists in the multiplying of the reflections and light points so that the sight is induced to
wander from point to point, and that forms and even
motions are suggested by the superposition and combination of the various reflections. Often, too, a light point
visible to one eye will not be so to the other, this sometimes provoking the phenomenon of binocular vision,
which asserts itself for a moment or two, when the
diverse images coalesce again, though imperfectly, giving an impression of movement. For one gifted with
imagination and the natural quality of visualizing brain-
pictures, these shifting light-points and the more or less
definite and repeated reflections of surrounding objects
offer abundant material out of which to construct life-
like pictures apparently seen in the crystal. That the
brain-pictures thus thrown out, so to speak, upon the
crystal, may or may not have a peculiar psychic value,
other than their value as mere phenomena, depends upon
the significance we are inclined to attribute to the processes of the subconscious intelligence; of its existence,
indeed, there can be no doubt, and many of our best
thinkers incline to the belief that through it the narrow
limits of our personality are occasionally transcended.

The following history and description of a crystal
ball is given by John Aubrey (1626–1697):

I have here set down the figure of a consecrated Beryl—now in
the possession of Sir Edward Harley, Knight of the Bath, which

---

[29] Miscellanea graphica: Representations of Ancient Medieval and
Renaissance remains in the Possession of Lord Londesborough; introd.
by Thomas Wright, London, 1857, p. 81.

1, 2, 3. Rock-crystal spheres having portions of the surface ground so that they are rendered partially opaque.

4. Natural cross of rock-crystal. On dolomite, Ossining, New York.

he keeps in his closet at Brampton Bryan in Herefordshire amongst his Cimelia, which I saw there. It came first from Norfolk; a minister had it there, and a call was to be made with it. Afterwards a miller had it and he did work great cures with it (if curable), and in the Beryl they did see, either the receipt in writing, or else the herb. To this minister, the spirits or angels would appear openly, and because the miller (who was his familiar friend) one day happened to see them, he gave him the aforesaid Beryl and Call; by these angels the minister was forewarned of his death. This account I had from Mr. Ashmole. Afterwards this Beryl came into somebody's hand in London who did tell strange things by it; insomuch that at last he was questioned for it, and it was taken away by authority (it was about 1645). This Beryl is a perfect sphere, the diameter of it I guess to be something more than an inch; it is set in a ring, or circle, of silver, resembling the meredian of a globe; the stem of it is about ten inches high, all gilt. At the four quarters of it are the names of four angels, viz: Uriel, Raphael, Michael, Gabriel. On the top is a cross patee.[30]

In his "Sudducismus Triumphatus," Joseph Glanvil writes that "one Compton of Summersetshire, who practised Physick, and pretends to strange Matters," demonstrated his power to evoke the image of a distant person on the surface of a mirror. Glanvil relates that Compton offered to show to a Mr. Hill any one the latter wished to see. Hill "had no great confidence in his talk," but replied that he desired to see his wife who was many miles distant. "Upon this, Compton took up a Looking-glass that was in the Room, and setting it down again, bid my Friend look in it, which he did, and then, as he most solemnly and seriously professeth, he saw the exact Image of his Wife, in that Habit which she then wore and working at her Needle in such a part of the Room (then represented also) in which and about which time she really was, as he found upon enquiry when he came

---

[30] Aubrey, "Miscellanies," London, 1890, pp. 156, 157. (There is a figure on p. 156.)

home. The Gentleman himself averred this to me, and he is a very sober, intelligent, and credible Person. Compton had no knowledge of him before, and was an utter stranger to the Person of his Wife. He was by all accounts a very odd Person.'' [31]

A contemporary record recites that when a certain Sir Marmaduke Langdale (of the seventeenth century) was in Italy, he went to a sorcerer and was shown in a glass his own figure kneeling before a crucifix. Though a Protestant at this time, he shortly after became a Catholic.[32] If we exclude all idea of trickery, it is likely enough that the idea of becoming a Catholic was already present to the scryer's mind and called up this picture before him.

The celebrated Cagliostro, a Sicilian whose real name was Giuseppe Balsamo, among his other arts to excite curiosity and play upon the superstition of his contemporaries, had recourse to a species of crystal-gazing. In the only authentic biography of this extraordinary impostor occurs the following passage, which we give in Carlyle's version: [33]

Cagliostro brought a little Boy into the Lodge, son of a nobleman there. He placed him on his knees before a table, whereon stood a Bottle of pure water, and behind this some lighted candles: he made an exorcism round the boy, put his hand on his head and both, in this attitude, addressed their prayers to God for the happy accomplishment of the work. Having bid the child look into the Bottle, directly the child cried that he saw a garden. Knowing hereby that Heaven assisted him, Cagliostro took courage, and bade the child ask of God the grace to see the angel Michael. At first the child said: "I see some-

---

[31] Glanvil, " Sadducismus Triumphatus," London, 1726, p. 281.

[32] Aubrey, " Miscellanies," London, 1890, p. 155.

[33] Carlyle, " Works," Ashburton ed., vol. xvi, p. 509; from Vie de Joseph Balsamo, traduite d'après l'original Italien, ch. ii, 111 (Paris, 1791).

thing white; I know not what it is." Then he began jumping, stamping like a possessed creature, and cried: "There now! I see a child like myself, that seems to have something angelical." All the assembly, and Cagliostro himself, remained speechless with emotion. . . . The child being anew exorcised with the hand of the Venerable on his head, and the customary prayer addressed to Heaven, he looked into the Bottle, and said he saw his sister at that moment coming down stairs, and embracing one of her brothers. That appeared impossible, the brother in question being then hundreds of miles off; however, Cagliostro felt not disconcerted; said they might send to the country-house where the sister was, and see.

Taken all in all this experiment does not seem very satisfactory; but we have in it all the essential phases of crystal-gazing. Excitement and expectation produced their usual effect upon an impressionable child, and suggestion did the rest; the final vision may have been corroborated in some way, or, if not, it would be explained so as to convince those present at the experiment that the child had really seen a representation of some actual happening.

During the Terror, among those upon whom fell the suspicions of the Jacobins was General Marlière. He knew that a trial and quite probably a condemnation awaited him. A few days before the date fixed for his appearance before his judges, he met a colonel in the French army, who had served in the American Revolutionary War, and who was a firm believer in the truth of the visions seen in crystal balls. In the course of the conversation this subject was alluded to, and the general immediately declared that he was eager to put the matter to the test, and learn, if possible, what fate was in store for him. The colonel was at first very unwilling to undertake the experiment, probably he thought that General Marlière's doom was sealed, and, believing as he did in the revelations of the crystal, he dreaded the results; however, the general insisted and the experiment took place. As usual, the medium was an "innocent child." In the crystal appeared a man wearing a private's uniform of the National Guard struggling with one wearing a general's uniform. The child was much excited and terrified by the sight, exclaiming that the general's assailant had thrown him down and was beheading him. That the vision portended the general's execution was clear enough, but the peculiar dress of the executioner was a mystery to those present at the test, for the official garb bore no resemblance whatever to a soldier's uniform. The prediction was, however, fulfilled to the letter. General Marlière was tried, found guilty, and guillotined. This in itself did not mean much in view of the innumerable executions in the time of the Terror; but, on the day of this execution, Samson, the official executioner, desiring to gratify his personal vanity and to attract the gaze of the spectators, dressed himself in the uniform of a national guardsman.[34] That this altogether unusual circumstance, which could scarcely have been known to any of those who assisted at the crystal-gazing, should have been revealed in the crystal, is certainly very mysterious. If we had positive assurance that the events narrated happened exactly in the way they are said to have happened, this would be one of the few instances in which the vision seen in the crystal reproduced something entirely unknown to the scryer.

Many extraordinary visions are said to have been seen in crystal balls by a French scryer whose grandmother had clairvoyant powers and was sometimes consulted by Napoleon I. It is claimed that the grandson

---

[34] Kiesewetter, "Faust in der Geschichte und Tradition," Leipzig, 1893, p. 476.

has enjoyed the patronage of many royal personages, and had predicted, in a more or less definite way, the assassination of King Humbert of Italy, and the attempted assassination of Alfonso XIII and of his young bride, when they were returning to the palace after the conclusion of the marriage ceremony. This French scryer has stated that he is powerfully affected when he is consulted by any one destined to die a violent death; on such occasions he feels, in his own organism, a modified form of the particular kind of suffering they are fated to experience. This exceptional sensitiveness to occult influences was also shown when the crystal-gazer went to the Boulaq Museum in Cairo, and gazed upon the rows of mummies exhibited there; he immediately felt, as intensely as though it were a personal experience, the mingled sorrow and rage of the disembodied spirits at seeing their embalmed bodies exposed to the view of the idle crowd, when they should have been permitted to rest in their tombs until the hour of the Resurrection.

In England all those who attempted, with a greater or less degree of success, to reveal the hidden secrets of the future, were expressly designated as rogues and vagabonds according to the terms of an act passed June 21, 1824.[35] Such offenders, on being duly convicted before the Justice of the Peace, could be committed to the House of Correction, "there to be kept at hard Labour for any time not exceeding Three Calendar Months." This class of undesirable citizens comprised all using "any subtle Craft, Means, or Device, by Palmistry or otherwise" for the deception of his Majesty's subjects.

The *h'men*, or diviner, of Yucatan, places great re-

---

[35] George IV, cap. lxxxiii.

liance upon his *zaztun,* or "clear stone." This may be a quartz crystal, or else some other translucent stone; but in order to serve for divining purposes it must be sanctified according to special rites, gum-copal being burned before it, and certain magic formulas recited, which have been transmitted from generation to generation in an archaic dialect. When thus rendered fit for use, the diviner claims to be able to see in the depths of the crystal the whereabouts of lost articles, and also what absent persons are doing at the time he makes his observation. Not only this, but the future is also laid bare before his eyes. As these stones are supposed to possess such miraculous powers we need not be surprised that one of them should be found in almost every village in Yucatan.[36]

The Apache medicine-men are also fully persuaded that crystals possess the virtue of inducing visions, and they have used them for the purpose of finding lost property. To aid in the recovery of stolen ponies is one of the most important tasks of the Apache medicine-man, and to this end his crystal offers great assistance. Capt. John G. Burke relates that he made a great friend of a medicine-man named Na-a-che by giving him a large crystal of denticulated spar, much superior to the crystal he had been in the habit of using for his visions. That this was thoroughly satisfactory to the medicine-man at least, is shown by his statement to Capt. Burke that by looking into his crystal he could see everything he wanted to see. Of the way this came about he did not attempt any explanation.[37]

---

[36] Brinton, " Essays of an Americanist," Philadelphia, 1890, p. 165.

[37] Burke, " The Medicine-men of the Apache," Ninth Annual Report of the Bureau of Ethnology, 1887–1888, Washington, 1892, p. 461.

The magic power supposed to dwell within rock-crystal has been recognized in a peculiar way by some natives of New South Wales. They have the barbarous custom of knocking out one or more of the front teeth of their boys at the obligatory initiation ceremonies, and on one occasion Dr. Howitt was entrusted with the care of a number of these teeth, which are believed to preserve a certain undefined connection with the health and fortunes of their former possessors, and on this account great fear was expressed lest the custodian should place the precious teeth in the same bag with some rock-crystals, for the natives thought that the magic power of these crystals would injuriously affect the teeth, and through them the boys, from whose jaws they had been broken.[38]

In a paper entitled "The Origin of Jewelry," read before the British Association, Professor W. Ridgeley says:

Australians and tribes of New Guinea use crystals for rain-making, although they cannot bore them, and this stone is a powerful amulet in Uganda when fastened into leather. Sorcerers in Africa carry a small bag of pebbles as an important part of their equipment. So it was in Greece. The crystal was used to light the sacrificial fire and was so employed in the church down to the fifteenth century. Egyptians used it largely under the XII Dynasty, piercing it along its axis after rubbing off the pyramid points of the crystal, sometimes leaving the natural six sides, or else grinding it into a complete cylinder. From this bead came the artificial cylindrical glass beads made later by the Egyptians.

Professor Ridgeley believes that the primary use of all these objects was because of their supposed magic powers. He holds the same view in regard to cylinders and rings, considering that the use of these as signets

---

[38] Fraser, " The Golden Bough," pt. i, " The Magic Art," vol. i, London, 1911, p. 176.

only became habitual at a later time, and he finds a proof of this theory in the fact that unengraved Babylonian cylinders and Mycenean gems have been discovered. This is, of course, perfectly true, but does not in the least prove that such ornaments may not have been originally worn simply for purposes of adornment; unquestionably, the custom of engraving them so as to render them signets must have arisen at a much later date.

Flacourt stated that the natives of Madagascar used crystals to aid them in divining. These stones, which were said to have fallen from heaven, were attached to the corners of the boards whereon the sorcerers produced their geomantic figures.[39]   Here, however, the crystals were not directly used, but were only supposed to attract influences propitious to the diviner's efforts.

In the notes to the 1888 edition of the Chinese criminal code, some curious details are given of a practice called Yuan-kuang-fuchou (the magic of the round glittering). While this designation certainly seems to indicate the use of a polished sphere of some description, the details given refer to a different practice. We are told that when anything was stolen appeal was sometimes made to a certain Sun-Yuan Sheng, who would then hang up a piece of white paper and utter a spell, while a boy gazed upon the paper until he saw the figure of the thief. This magician was punished for carrying on an unlawful practice.[40]

The Mexicans made images of their god Tezcatlipoca of obsidian, and the name of this divinity is interpreted as signifying "shining mirror." This is supposed to refer to, or to have been expressed by, the brilliant effect

---

[39] Lang, " The Making of Religion," London, 1898, pp. 91–92.
[40] Thomas, " Crystal Gazing," London, 1905, p. 48.

BABYLONIAN CYLINDERS AND PERSIAN BEADS.

hematite, rock-crystal, lapis-lazuli, chalcedony, banded agate, and other stones.   From 3000 B.C. to the Christian era.   (See page 121.)

of the polished surface of the obsidian. Mirrors of this material are said to have been used for divination in ancient Mexico and the neighboring countries.[41] One of these Mexican mirrors seems to have been employed by Dr. Dee in his experiments in crystal vision.

A remarkable series of tests in the art of scrying, given in the presence of Lane, the great Arabic scholar, and translator of the Arabian Nights, illustrates the fallibility of most of the evidence adduced in such matters, for, at first, Lane was strongly impressed by the exhibition. Although no crystal was used, the process of scrying was precisely the same as in crystal-gazing,—that is to say, the vision called for by the visitors was seen by the scryer on a polished surface. The master of ceremonies was an Arab magician, though, of course, he did not do the scrying himself, but employed a boy for this purpose, for it is generally thought that half-grown boys or girls are more receptive. Although Lane himself was perfectly familiar with Arabic, an interpreter was always present in the interest of the other Europeans who assisted at the experiments.

After invoking many mysterious geniuses and burning incense and scraps of paper inscribed with magic formulas, the magician drew a magic square on a large sheet of paper and dropped a quantity of ink in the centre. On this the boy was directed to fix his gaze, and after he had shown that he was thoroughly under the magician's influence, by describing the images suggested to him, the visitors were permitted to ask him questions. The answers were successful in most cases; a single instance will suffice. When the boy was asked to describe Admiral

41 Nuttall, " The Fundamental Principles of Old and New World Civilization," Cambridge, Mass., 1901, p. 80.

Nelson, he replied: "I see a man clothed in a dark garb; there is something strange about him, he has but one arm." Then, quickly correcting himself, he added: "No, I was mistaken, he has one of his arms across his breast." This correction impressed those present more than the first statement, for it was well known that Nelson usually had the empty sleeve of his coat pinned to his breast. It also seemed as though there could be no collusion, for both the magician and the boy were ignorant of everything English and evidently knew nothing of Nelson. Unfortunately, however, for those who would fain believe that there is something supernatural in scrying, it was later discovered that the interpreter was a renegade Scotchman, masquerading as an Arab, and there can be little doubt that he managed to suggest the boy's answer. The fact that no satisfactory results were obtained when this interpreter was absent, makes this explanation almost certainly the correct one.

The Armenians sometimes practised divination by watching the images that appeared, or were supposed to appear, on the smooth surface of the waters of a well, and the person who saw such images was called *hornaiogh*, "he who looks into a well." An Arab woman living in the neighborhood of Constantinople enjoyed a great reputation for her power in this respect, and was frequently consulted by Armenians and by other dwellers in the Turkish capital. Whoever wished to question this woman regarding the cause of an illness, the whereabouts of stolen objects, etc., usually took along a child of the household, and the actual scrying was generally performed by this child, who would describe or identify the forms it saw on the water's surface. If, however, for one reason or another, no child was brought, the witch herself did the scrying. In regard to illness, a distinction was made between "natural" maladies and those directly caused by some spirit. Should the spirit (*peri*) supposed to cause the dire malady known as *drsévé,* a kind of consumption, be seen to glide over the surface of the water, the sorceress would find it necessary to invoke the whole race of *peris* to come to the aid of the patient, who was expected to pay more than the usual fee for this very special service.[42]

The *peris* of Armenian legend were sometimes good and sometimes evil spirits; in the former case these were supposed to perform the functions of guardian angels, and every one was said to have a peri especially delegated to watch over him. This found expression in the fact that when one Armenian felt at first sight an instinctive sympathy for another, he would say, "My peri loves you dearly (*peris chad siretz kezi*)." In the contrary case, the feeling of antipathy was also attributed to the attitude assumed by the guardian spirit toward the new acquaintance.[43] These spirits were therefore supposed to encourage or discourage greater intimacy with newcomers in accord with the true interests of those over whom they watched.

The power to see images in a crystal does not appear to depend to any great extent upon a morbid nervous condition of the seer, for many of the most successful experimenters have been of good and even of exceptionally vigorous physique. Indeed, illness seems to diminish or destroy this power, at least in the case of those who are habitually healthy.[44] This does not imply that some highly nervous and even hysterical individuals have not

[42] Tcheraz, "Notes sur la mythologie Arménéenne," in Trans. of the Ninth Cong. of Orient. (1892), London, 1893, vol. ii, p. 832.

[43] Tcheraz, l. c., p. 835.

[44] Proc. Soc. of Psych. Research, vol. viii, p. 470.

been favored with "crystal visions." Very probably the rule here is the same as in ordinary hypnotism. Those persons who have a strong will and sound nerves are able to hypnotize themselves, while those whose nerves are disordered are subject to the hypnotic influence of others.

A well-known lady in New York City, in conversation with the writer, a few years ago, on the subject of crystal balls, was advised by him to try a ball herself and see what results she obtained. At the end of two years she found that by concentration she had been able to better her understanding of herself; and this effect is not only obtainable now by means of a crystal ball, but by fixing her gaze upon any bright object. This visual fixation has centred her whole being in such a way that her health has notably improved.

What are the laws that govern the production of these phenomena? That the "visions" are real enough has been proven time and again, but it seems almost certain that they do not offer anything but the ideas or impressions existing in the minds or optic nerves of the gazers. One of the most painstaking students of the subject, Miss Goodrich-Freer, gives many instances in proof of this, which show how easy it would be for a less critical observer to suppose that the crystal revealed something unknown to the gazer. On one occasion this lady was at a loss to remember the correct address of a friend whose letter, received a few days before, she had torn up. She resorted to her crystal, and after a few minutes saw in it, in gray letters on a white ground, the address she had forgotten. She mailed her answer to this address, and the reply came duly to hand, with the address stamped in gray upon the white paper of the note, which was

identical with that she had first received.[45]   The visual
impression had been stirred up and "externalized" itself
when she gazed upon the crystal.   We believe that this
explains the larger number of such visions, and that the
rest are only inexplicable because the scryer has forgotten the source of the impression that is projected on
the surface of the crystal.

It is true that both Miss Goodrich-Freer and many
other crystal-gazers note instances in which the vision
appears to represent something the scryer does not and
cannot know.   However, even in these cases, when carefully examined, there is little difficulty in finding an explanation.   Coincidence accounts for much, and imagination for more, since it is not the vision itself, but the
memory of the vision, that is later brought into comparison with actual facts.   We all know how exceedingly hard
it is to repeat, after a short lapse of time, all the circumstances and details of any occurrence.   There is a natural
growth and modification of mental impressions, due to
association of ideas, and where there exists the least wish
to make the prophecy accord with the event, or the vision
with the coincident happening, this growth and modification will be in the direction of agreement.   This takes
place quite unconsciously, and the informant will be fully
persuaded that all the circumstances are related exactly
as they occurred.

The attempt to identify either persons or scenes observed by the scryer with real persons and real scenes
unknown to him, must always be open to the objection
that the one who makes the identification has no photo-
graphic impression upon which to base his judgment, but
merely the words of the scryer.   When we remember

---

[45] Proc. of the Soc. for Psych. Research, vol. v, p. 507.

14

what mistakes have been made in identifying individuals from photographs, we can easily appreciate the great chances of error entailed by the use of a verbal description of a visionary experience, even when the person giving the description is both willing and able to make it as exact and adequate as possible.

A very impartial witness, Andrew Lang, states that, in the course of a series of experiments he made in crystal-gazing, he saw nothing himself, but found that a surprisingly large proportion of those who tried were successful in seeing pictures of some sort on the polished surface. Almost invariably, when the gazer fixed his eyes upon the sphere, it appeared to grow milky-hued and then became black; upon this dark background the pictures showed themselves. One of the scryers, a lady, said that as a child she had seen pictures in ink that she had spilled for the purpose.[46] This method has been much favored by Orientals. While Lang does not quite venture to assert that all the "visions" reported to him were genuine ones, he inclines to the belief that this was the case with many of them. Experience has shown, however, that not all of those who see pictures in, or on, a glass or crystal sphere, can also see them in ink.[47] Nevertheless, in view of the fact that the crystal sphere is said to appear black to the eye before the pictures are seen, it would seem that some naturally black surface would be particularly adapted for the purpose.

An interesting point regarding the phenomena of crystal-gazing is the effect produced by magnification upon the images seen in, or on, the crystal ball. As to

[46] Thomas, "Crystal Gazing," London, 1908, Lang's preface, pp. xi, xii.
[47] Thomas, l. c., p. xxi.

this matter there is considerable difference of opinion, for, while some experimenters assert that the interposition of a magnifying-glass enlarges the image, others have not remarked any difference in its size under these conditions. Indeed, one of the most critical witnesses, Mrs. A. W. Verrall, declares that her vision entirely disappeared when she held a magnifying-glass before her eyes. On the other hand, we have the case of a subject who had been told, while in the hypnotic state, that he would see a play-bill on the crystal. When he was awakened and the crystal ball was placed before him, he said that he could see only detached letters, but when he looked through a magnifying-glass he saw all the letters distinctly and read the name of the play, in perfect accord with the suggestion.[48]

This image may have been reflected from some part of the room where the gazer had not noticed it, and may have been either before or behind the operator. The magnifying-glass would naturally make the small, condensed letters legible, as a play-bill would be many times larger than a crystal ball, and its minute image naturally too small to read, being reduced by the circular surface.

Usually, however, the image is not on the surface of the crystal, but in the beholder's eye; therefore when this image appears more clearly under magnification, the result is due to the expectation of the gazer based upon his experience of an invariable rule. This acts as a stimulus upon the visual function, which must be in an exceedingly sensitive state to produce visions at all. When, however, no result or a negative result follows the use of the glass, then we can safely assume that

---

[48] Proc. of the Soc. for Psych. Research, vol. viii, p. 473.

the gazer was naturally of a critical turn of mind, and was disposed to distrust sensual impressions; hence the glass became a disturbing influence, interfering with or even completely obliterating the eye-picture.

Many attempts have been made to establish distinctions between the different materials used for crystals, proceeding on the theory that subtle emanations from them affected the gazer and played an important part in producing the desired vision.   That the beryl produced a greater number of these visions than any other mineral was the old belief which is still upheld in some quarters to-day; one scryer, indeed, asserts that his clearest and most satisfactory visions were seen in a cube of blue beryl, the beautiful color appearing to dispose the soul to a harmonious unfolding of its latent aptitudes.[49]

Among the instructions given to a would-be crystal gazer, the question of a proper and wholesome diet is not overlooked, as anything which tends to disturb the serenity of the organism will also interfere with the due exercise of the special clairvoyant faculty that expresses itself in crystal visions.   A curious special recommendation made by one of the exponents of the art is that good results can be had by drinking an infusion of mugwort (*Artemisia vulgaris*), or of chicory (*Cichorium intybus*), because of their tonic and antibilious qualities. Moreover, we are told that these herbs are under the influence of the zodiacal sign Libra, the sign controlling the virtues of the beryl.[50]   Above all the portion of the lunar month when the moon is on the increase is said to be far the best season for scrying, as the old astrologers recognized an affinity between the moon and rock-crystal.

---

[49] Shepharial, " The Crystal and the Seer," London [1900?], p. 14.
[50] John Melville, " Crystal Gazing," London, 1910, pp. 20, 21.

ROCK-CRYSTAL SPHERES. JAPANESE. (See page 217.)

The claim is made that the adept at crystal-gazing can determine by the apparent difference in proximity of the visions whether they refer to the present or to a more or less remote past or future, that is to say, are nearer or farther removed in time from the period when the vision appears. The distinction between past and future is admitted to offer greater difficulty and a decision as to this point must depend upon a kind of intuitive and undefined impression on the part of the scryer.

Those who have made a sympathetic study of crystal-gazing recognize that the "visions" seen in or on the crystal differ according to the mental and psychic temperament of the scryer. Two broad distinctions are sometimes established, the one class comprising those whose mental attitude is a "positive" one while the second class includes the "passive" subjects. In the former case the crystal visions are more apt to be symbols denoting some past or future event than a clear picture of the event itself, the mentality of the "positive" subject being, perhaps, too strong merely to mirror the image cast upon it. Instead of so doing it transforms the impression received from this image into some symbolic form. This process is not, however, consciously done, but the scryer of this type is supposed nevertheless to have an instinctive appreciation of the fact that what he sees is purely and simply a symbol, and he proceeds to interpret this in accord with certain generally received rules, or in accord with his own personal experience.

The passive subject on the other hand is more apt to see a clear and definite picture of the persons or events revealed to him. Sometimes that picture is distinctly perceptible on or about the surface of the crystal, while at other times the visual perception will be rather indefinite and clouded, although accompanied by a strong mental impression in itself equivalent to that which would have been induced by an actual and objective vision.[51]

The proper use of the crystal is the prime factor in the art of scrying and great attention is paid to this point by all those who treat seriously of the subject. Among other things they recognize that freedom from pain, or even from a sense of physical discomfort, is quite essential, for the mind must assume a purely passive and receptive attitude, and not be forced to take cognizance of bodily discomfort. Moreover the nervous system must be in repose, for which reason a reasonable time should be allowed to lapse after taking a meal, before trying for crystal visions.[52]

An author on "psychomancy" affirms that fixing the gaze upon a crystal ball is one of the very best means of bringing out the latent faculty of astral vision, and he finds a reason for this in the atomic structure, the molecular arrangement of the material. He does not, however, impart any definite information as to what special structural characteristics render glass or rock-crystal particularly efficient in this direction.[53] The help that may be derived from crystal-gazing by those who are striving to pierce the veil that separates the "real life" about us from that spiritual life which is so much more real for those who believe in it, is also admitted by many.[54]

We cannot refrain from citing here the words spoken by Sir Oliver Lodge at Birmingham, Sept. 10, 1913, before the British Association for the Advancement of Science,

---

[51] Shepharial, "The Crystal and the Seer," London [1900?] pp. 11–13.

[52] Melville, "Crystal Gazing," London, 1910, p. 47.

[53] Atkinson, "Practical Psychomancy and Crystal Gazing," Chicago [1908], p. 46.

[54] See Leadbeater, "The Astral Plane," London, 1910, p. 14.

affirming his conviction, as a result of scientific investigation of occult phenomena, ''that memory and affection
are not limited to that association with matter by which
alone they can manifest themselves here and now, and
that personality persists beyond bodily death.''

One of the latest types of glass balls for crystal-gazing has a small, circular, flat surface on the sphere. This
may possibly be of service in furnishing a better field for
the expected vision, and may also lessen the troublesome
and baffling reflections which interfere so seriously with
the projection of the mental picture.

A method that has been recommended to crystal-
gazers is to place the crystal on a table, protect it from
the reflections of surrounding objects by means of a
velvet screen, and set seven candlesticks with wax tapers
in front of the screen. The tapers are then to be lighted,
the room being otherwise in perfect darkness, and the
would-be scryer is to seat himself comfortably before
the table, laying his hands flat upon it, and to gaze fixedly
upon the crystal for half an hour or longer. The light
from the tapers will certainly ensure a multitude of light
points in the crystal. That the molecules forming the
sphere may always remain *en rapport* with the gazer,
he is advised to put it beneath his pillow when retiring
to rest.[55]

The crystal gazer is strongly advised by some to limit
the duration of his experiment at first to five minutes,
during which he is to avoid thinking of anything in particular while keeping his eyes fixed intently upon the
ball, but without any undue straining of attention. Should
the eyes ''water'' after the test is concluded, this is to
be regarded as an indication that the gazer has persisted

---

[55] Verner, '' How to Know Your Future,'' London [1910?], p. 16.

too long; for brain-fag is to be strictly avoided, as such a state depresses instead of arousing the hidden and higher psychic faculties.   Even after considerable practice, the scrying should not be carried on for more than a few minutes at a time.   The faculty of visualization plays a most important part in crystal-gazing.   The image thought to be seen on, before, or behind the surface of the crystal, is in its essence a fancied projection of a purely mental image conceived in the brain; such an image as is present to the consciousness of many when they call to mind a scene of some vivid past experience, or the face of someone they have known, and *see* it as an element of consciousness.   When it is possible to externalize this interior vision, then we have at least a beginning of successful scrying.   That it may go far beyond this, that it may reveal to the gazer events happening in some distant place, or even events yet to transpire in the dim future, is often claimed.   An acceptance of this claim must depend largely upon our attitude toward premonitions and prophecies in general.   Here, as in the simple picture evolved by an image of the past, the crystal is merely the background upon which are cast the mind-pictures or soul-pictures arising within our being.[56]

A use of crystal gazing to aid literary composition has been reported in the case of an English authoress of note, who, if she lost the thread of the story she was writing, would resort to her crystal, and would see mirrored therein the scenes and personages of her tale, the latter carrying on the plot in dramatic action.   Aided by this suggestion she was able to resume her composition and successfully terminate her story.

---

[56] See Hereward Carrington's Correspondence Course of Instruction in Psychic Development, Lesson 24, New York, 1912.

CRYSTAL BALL, SUPPORTED BY BRONZE DRAGON. JAPANESE.

In Japan the smaller rock-crystals were believed to be the congealed breath of the White Dragon, while the larger and more brilliant ones were said to be the saliva of the Violet Dragon. As the dragon was emblematic of the highest powers of creation, this indicates the esteem in which the substance was held by the Japanese, who probably derived their appreciation of it from the Chinese. The name *suisho,* used both in China and Japan to designate rock-crystal, reflects the idea current in ancient times, and repeated even by seventeenth century writers, that rock-crystal was ice which had been so long congealed that it could not be liquefied.

For the Japanese, rock-crystal is the "perfect jewel," *tama;* it is at once a symbol of purity and of the infinity of space, and also of patience and perseverance. This latter significance probably originating from an observation of the patience and skill shown by the accurate and painstaking Japanese cutters and polishers of rock-crystal.

A crystal ball, one of the largest perfect spheres ever produced, has been made from rock-crystal of Madagascar. It is a very perfect sphere and of faultless material. The diameter is 6⅛ inches and the ball was held at about $20,000.

Many fine crystal balls are made in Japan, the materials being found in large, clear masses in the mountains on the islands of Nippon and Fusiyama and also in the granitic rocks of Central Japan. It is stated, however, that much of the Japanese material really comes from China. The Japanese methods of working rock-crystals are extremely simple and depend more upon the skill and patience of the workers than upon the tools at their command. Our illustration, taken from a sketch made by an Oriental traveller, shows the process of manufacturing crystal balls. The rough mass of crystal is gradually rounded by careful chipping with a small steel hammer. With the aid of this tool alone a perfect sphere is formed. The Japanese workmen thoroughly understand the fracture of the mineral, and know just when to apply chipping and when hammering. The crystal, having been reduced to a spherical form, is handed to a grinder, whose tools consist of cylindrical pieces of cast iron, about a foot in length, and full of perforations. These cylinders are of different curvatures, according to the size of the crystal to be ground. Powdered emery and garnet are used for the first polishing. Plenty of water is supplied during the process, and the balls are kept constantly turning, in order to secure a true spherical surface. Sometimes they are fixed on the end of a hollow tube and kept dexterously turning in the hand until smooth. The final polishing is effected with crocus or rouge (finely divided hematite), giving a splendid lustrous surface. As hand labor is exclusively used, the manufacture of crystal objects according to the Japanese methods is extremely laborious and slow.[57]

In Germany and France and in the United States, the fabrication of rock-crystal is accomplished almost entirely by machinery. The crystal to be shaped into a ball is placed against a semicircular groove worn in huge grindstones. This is illustrated in the case of the method practised in Oberstein, Germany. The workman has his feet firmly braced against a support, and, resting upon his chest, presses the crystal against the revolving grindstone. It is unnecessary to add that the practice is

---

[57] Kunz, " The Occurrence and Manipulation of Rock Crystal," Scientific American, vol. lv, pp. 103, 104 (Aug. 14, 1886). Trans. N. Y. Acad. Sciences, May 30, 1886.

METHOD OF GRINDING CRYSTAL BALLS AND OTHER HARD STONE
OBJECTS IN GERMANY AND FRANCE.

JAPANESE METHOD OF CHIPPING, GRINDING AND POLISHING
ROCK-CRYSTAL BALLS.

extremely unwholesome and develops early consumption among the workers. A constant stream of water is kept flowing over the stone so that the crystal shall always be moist, as the friction would otherwise hurt it, and the subsequent addition of water would be liable to cause a fracture. The final polishing is done on a wooden wheel with tripoli, or by means of a leather buffer with tripoli or rouge.[58]

There are three fine crystal balls in the collection of the American Museum of Natural History. One, apparently perfect, measures 5½ inches in diameter and was cut from a crystal found in Mokolumne, Calaveras Co., California; the second is 6½ inches in diameter and is from the same locality, but not entirely perfect. These were shown in the department of the Tiffany Collection prepared by the author, and were exhibited at the Paris Exposition of 1900 as part of the J. Pierpont Morgan gift to the American Museum of Natural History. Another fine crystal ball is now to be seen in the American Museum of Natural History, New York; this was donated to the institution. It measures $4^{11}/_{16}$ inches in diameter, is of wonderful purity, and the cutting has been executed with such a high degree of precision that an ideally perfect sphere has been produced.[59]

Crystal balls have been found occasionally in tombs or in funerary urns, and their presence in sepulchres may perhaps be considered to have been due to a belief that they possessed certain magic properties. In the tomb of Childeric (ca. 436–481 A.D.), the father of Clovis, a rock-crystal sphere was found which was for a time preserved in the Bibliothèque Royale, Paris, and later in

---

[58] Kunz, " The Occurrence and Manipulation of Rock Crystal."

[59] Gratacap, " The Mystic Crystal Sphere," in the American Museum Journal, January, 1913, p, 24; plate on p. 22.

tne Louvre Museum; it measures 1½ inches in diameter.[60]
The chance discovery of a number of crystal balls is related by Montfaucon. Towards the end of the sixteenth
century, the canons of San Giovanni in Laterano, Rome,
wished to have some repairs made to a house they owned,
just outside of the city walls, and sent thither some workmen with the order to break up or remove two large,
superimposed stones, which were much in the way. The
workmen proceeded to break the upper stone, but were
much astonished to find embedded within it an alabaster
funerary urn with its cover. This had been hidden between the two stones, a space for its reception having
been hollowed out in the upper and lower stones, so that
it fitted within them. Opening the urn there were found
inside, mingled with the ashes, twenty crystal balls, a
gold ring with a stone setting, a needle, an ivory comb,
and some bits of gold wire. The presence of the needle
was taken to indicate conclusively that the ashes were
those of a woman.[61]

The discovery of the tomb of Childeric was made,
May 27, 1653, by a deaf-mute mason, named Adrien
Quinquin, while he was excavating for the restoration of
one of the dependencies of the church of Saint Brice de
Tournai. One of the most interesting objects found in
the tomb was the golden signet of Childeric bearing his
head and the legend *Childerici regis*. The earliest
description is given in a work by Chiflet entitled "Anas-
tasis Childerici," "Resurrection of Childeric," published by Plantin of Antwerp in 1655. The various ornaments were sent by the Spanish Governor-General of the
Netherlands to the Austrian treasury in Vienna, and
were not long afterward, in 1664, graciously donated by

---

[60] Montfaucon, Les monumens de la monarchie Française, Paris,
1729, p. 15.
[61] Montfaucon, l. c.

ROCK-CRYSTAL SPHERE.

Japan, five inches diameter. Morgan collection, American Museum of Natural History, New York.

Emperor Leopold I to King Louis XIV, at the instance of Johann Philip of Schonborn, Archbishop of Mainz, who was under great obligation to the French sovereign.

In Paris the various ornaments were preserved in the Bibliothèque Royale until the night of November 5–6, 1831, when many of them, with other valuables, were stolen by an ex-convict. Closely pursued by the police, the thief threw his booty into the Seine; much of the plunder was subsequently recovered, but the signet of Childeric was lost for ever. The crystal ball had not seemed of sufficient value to tempt the thief and was left undisturbed; it was later, in 1852, deposited in the Louvre Museum.[62]

In a personal communication to Abbé Cochet made in 1858 by Mr. Thomas Wright, the latter stated that he had seen at Downing in Flintshire with Lord Fielding five crystal balls, bearing labels declaring that they came from the sepulchres of the kings of France violated at the time of the French Revolution. They had been purchased about 1810 at the sale of the Duchess of Portland's effects.[63]

Among the crystal balls found in French sepulchres may be noted one discovered by Rigollot in 1853 at Arras, and preserved in the Museum of that city; this still has the original gold mounting serving to attach it to the necklace from which it had been worn suspended. Another found at or near Levas was in the possession of M. Dancoise, a notary of Hénin-Liétard, dept. Pas de Calais.[64] In the Bibliothèque at Dieppe there is a crystal ball, 32 mm. in diameter, found at Douvrend, dept. Seine-Inferieure, in 1838, in a Merovingian tomb; this is pierced

---

[62] Cochet, " Le tombeau de Childeric Ier roi des Francs," Paris, 1859, pp. 16 sqq.

[63] Cochet, op. cit., p. 305.

[64] Cochet, op. cit., p. 302; figure.

through.[65] The department of Moselle supplied three discoveries of this kind, crystal balls having been found in a tomb at St. Preux-la-Montagne, Sablon and Moineville near Briey, the latter measuring 36 mm. in diameter.[66]

The Saxon tombs of England have also furnished a contingent of crystal balls, for example at Chatham, at Chassel Down on the Isle of Wight, where four were discovered, at Breach Down, Barham, near Canterbury, at Fairford, Gloucestershire, and also in Kent.[67]

We should also note a crystal ball found in a funerary urn at Hinsbury Hill, Northamptonshire;[68] this as well as the one found at Fairford was facetted.[69] From St. Nicholas, Worcestershire, is reported a crystal ball $1\frac{1}{2}$ inches in diameter.[70]

In his "Hydrotaphia, or Urn Burial," published in 1658, Sir Thomas Browne (1605–1682), author of the "Religio Medici," relates that there was at that time in the possession of Cardinal Farnese, an urn in which, besides a number of antique engraved gems, an ape of agate, and an elephant of amber, there had been found a crystal ball and six "nuts" of crystal.[71]

---

[65] Cochet, op. cit., p. 303, No. 1.

[66] Simon, " Observations sur les sépulchres antiques découverts dans plusieures contrées des Gaules," p. 5; pl. ii, fig. 14.

[67] See Wylie's Fairford Graves," pl. iv, fig. 1, pl. v, fig 2; Akerman's "Remains of Pagan Saxondom," Roach Smith's " Collectanea antiqua "; Douglas' "Nenia Brittanica," and Hillier's "Antiquities of the Isle of Wight."

[68] Akerman, op. cit., p. 10.

[69] Journal of the Archæological Institute, vol. ix, p. 179.

[70] Akerman, op. cit., pp. 39, 40.

[71] Miscellanies upon various subjects, by John Aubrey, to which is added "Hydrotaphia, or Urn Burial," by Sir Thomas Browne, London, 1890, p. 244; chap. ii.

One of the largest and most perfect crystal balls is in the Dresden "Grüne Gewölbe" (Green Vaults). This weighs 15 German pounds and measures 6 2/3 inches in diameter; it was undoubtedly used for purposes of augury. Ten thousand dollars was the price paid for it in 1780.

A crystal ball known as the Currahmore Crystal, because it is kept at the seat of that name belonging to the Marquis of Waterford, has long enjoyed and still enjoys the repute of possessing magical powers. It is of rock-crystal, and the legend runs that one of the Le Poers brought it from the Holy Land, where it had been given him by the great crusader Godefroy de Bouillon (1058–1100). The ball is a trifle larger than an orange and a silver ring encircles it at the middle. The chief and much-prized virtue of this crystal is its power to cure cattle of any one of the many distempers to which they are subject. Its application for this purpose is rather peculiar, for the cattle are not touched with it, but driven up and down a stream in which it has been laid. Not only in the immediate neighborhood of Currahmore is resort had to this magic stone by the peasants, but requests for its loan are often made from far distant parts of Ireland. The privilege is almost always accorded and has never been abused, the crystal being in every case conscientiously returned to its rightful owner.[72]

The names "ghost-crystals," "phantom-crystals," "spectre-crystals," "shadow-crystals," etc., are applied to a form of quartz in which the crystallization was interrupted from time to time, so that in the transparent successive layers there is an occasional opaque layer,

---

[72] Lady Wilde, "Ancient Legends, Mystic Charms, and Superstitions of Ireland," Boston, 1888, p. 209.

often no thicker than the finest possible dusting of a whiter material. Sometimes as many as fifteen or twenty of these successive growths are observable, one over the other. When these crystals are in the natural form, they show beautifully from the sides and ends. Sometimes such crystals are found after they have been rolled in the beds of mountain torrents until they have become entirely opaque, but when the surfaces are polished, the "phantom," "spectre," or "ghost," appears with wonderful beauty. Occasionally the entire crystal has been worn down to a small part of the original prism, in which case it is cut into a ball. The ball may seem to be absolutely pure, but when held in certain lights little tent-like markings can often be observed; sometimes only one marking is visible, but there may be as many as twenty. These are occasionally due to a layer of smoky material, and, though they add a charm to the ball, they detract from its value. Nevertheless, crystal-gazers may find an additional interest when the "ghostly" or "spectral" interior exists in a crystal ball. This growth is similar in kind to that seen at times in opaque quartz, forming what is known as cap-quartz; here the crystallizations can frequently be broken apart so that they fit one over the other in many successive layers. Occasionally the regular crystalline development will be interrupted, as it were, and in place of the original crystal continuing its growth harmoniously, a larger crystal will form on a smaller one, forming a sort of mushroom, or "cap," or "stilt" quartz, as it is termed.